EXPLORING CAREERS
IN THE MILITARY
SERVICES

EXPLORING CAREERS IN THE MILITARY SERVICES

by

Robert W. Macdonald

THE ROSEN PUBLISHING GROUP

New York

Published in 1987 by The Rosen Publishing Group
29 East 21st Street, New York, NY 10010

First Edition

Library of Congress Cataloging-in-Publication Data

Macdonald, Robert W.
  Exploring careers in the military services.

  (Exploring careers)
  Includes index.
  1. United States—Armed Forces—Vocational
guidance. I. Title. II. Series: Exploring
careers (Rosen Publishing Group)
  UB147.M324   1987   355'.0023'73   86-31553
  ISBN 0-8239-0694-9

Manufactured in the United States of America

Contents

About the Author

ROBERT W. MACDONALD retired as a Lieutenant Colonel after more than thirty years of Regular Army and Army Reserve service that he began as an infantry rifleman and ended as a Visiting Professor at the Army War College. When he retired, in 1975, Colonel Macdonald was awarded the Army's Meritorious Service Medal for "outstandingly meritorious service as a Citizen Soldier."

Mustered out of the Army as Staff Sergeant in 1945, Macdonald had barely finished college when he was back in uniform as a Reserve officer, during the Korean War. The tour of duty stretched into nearly a decade of active service and a Regular commission, before he left the Army to pursue a civilian career—armed once again with a Reserve commission. Army assignments in the United States and Europe had meanwhile given him unique opportunities to work with several branches of the Army and elements of other military services. Army Reserve activities later broadened this exposure.

In his civilian role, Colonel Macdonald has been an educator, a social science researcher, a business executive, and a diplomat. Besides broad military schooling, ranging from basic training to Command and General Staff College, he holds a doctorate in International Relations and has lectured and published in that field.

Colonel Macdonald resides in Colorado Springs, Colorado. When not actively engaged in research, writing, or teaching, he is likely to be found on a nearby ski slope or sailing on the Chesapeake Bay, depending on the season.

Preface

Once upon a time, a young man I knew well was sitting quietly in a room, listening. The room was just far enough from the chaos of the main processing center that he could understand ordinary conversation without straining. So, he listened. Quietly, without appearing to be hearing anything.

It was warm in the room, and the air was full of the stink of moth-balls from the wrinkled olive drab uniforms that everyone wore. But it was good. The young man had been cold for the past four hours as he was shunted from office to office, building to building, and handed uniforms, forms to fill out, tests to take. Cold, and hungry. It was good to be warm. He listened quietly to the talk of the other men down the row of chairs.

"I'm going to OCS at Benning," one young man confided to his neighbor. "I'm a college grad, you know. What about you?"

"Me? Well I've been shanghaied, that's what," the other man said. "Already enlisted for the Navy but the stupid draft board sent me here anyway. Look, I got the papers right here. See?" He held up an official-looking envelope.

"You're shanghaied, you'll get out of it," another bright-looking kid chimed in. "I'm a fourth-year ROTC cadet. Damned if they get me as a private. Nothing less than second lieutenant, I say."

"Fourth-year ROTC? What do you know? I put in two hitches in the Marines," said another. "China," he grunted, as if that explained everything, then he shut up and stared into space. "Damn," he muttered after a while. "I want out of this pansy Army."

"College kids!" An older-looking man had been listening but saying nothing. "Listen," he said now, "I got a license as a tugboat captain. I done my time in the Navy, too. Think I want to be a foot-sloggin' rifle-totin', mud-eatin' dogface? Not on your life."

The young man listened quietly. And he heard everything. One by one the others were called in for interviews behind closed doors. One by one they came out smiling. When the tugboat captain came out, he walked over to the two college boys.

"Gotcha!" He grinned at them. "You college kids! Wet behind the ears, you are. Second johns get their heads blown off too," he roared at them, from behind a big grin. "Me, I'm going to drive a tugboat. Right in New York harbor. Be home every night for supper with the ol' lady." He rolled his eyes at the college kids. "Now, what d'ya think about that, college kids?"

The man suddenly sobered. "Well, I feel sorry for you guys," he said. "Next week, you'll be crawling through the mud under barbed wire, while I'm drinkin' a coupla beers with me buddies on the docks."

"Master sergeant!" he grinned. "That's what they're gonna make me. Master Sergeant Eddie Finnegan! Nice ring to it, no?"

He turned and walked out of the room. As he passed, the young man could hear him muttering to himself: "Second looies! Think they own the world!"

Then the young recruit had his turn. The prearranged assignment to the special unit that was just being formed was confirmed. He was satisfied that it had worked out. But as he walked out of the room into the din of the main processing hall, he was also puzzled.

Some of the new words he had heard puzzled him, that is. What did the college kid mean by ROTC? What was OCS? And, then, why did an old ex-Marine expect to get special treatment? Why did the Army need tugboat captains? Or tugboats? What was a second john, anyway? The young man decided that he had a lot to learn about the Army.

And, eventually, he did learn. The hard way. Basic training, advanced individual training in communications, noncommissioned officer's school, and a jump to sergeant. More training.

The officers in the unit came and went. The new ones were mostly kids just out of Officer Candidate School at Ft. Benning, which he now knew was the Infantry Center, in Georgia. Some others were college graduates who got their commissions through the Reserve Officers Training Corps program, ROTC for short. They needed a lot of help from the sergeant. But they eventually became leaders of men.

Then combat. As the Army harbor tug eased the troopship out of the harbor, someone leaned out of the pilothouse door and waved. Eddy Finnegan? Probably not. But Eddie knew something that our friend should have known. Well, our friend had learned a lot by now. The hard way.

A fairy tale? Hardly. I was the young man on that cold January morning many long years ago. I often think about those other men in the waiting room at the military processing center. Of course they knew something I didn't. A lot, in fact, that I learned the hard way—and made mistakes while I was learning.

This book should be dedicated to those young men, whom I never saw again. But it isn't.

The Army and the other military services have changed a lot since those days. But, as the French say, "The more things change, the more they are the same." You can learn a lot about the things that puzzled me after I enlisted in the Army. So, in another way, this book is dedicated to you and all young readers who may be wondering what military service is all about and whether they should take a chance and try it for a while.

Most of the changes in the military services in recent years have been for the better because they reflect the society that surrounds and nourishes them. Life in the military can be exciting and it can be deadly dull, but it need never be uninteresting if you know what you are doing.

Read the book. Ask questions of everybody—your parents, your guidance counselor, your teachers, maybe even the local recruiting sergeant. The more you know before you raise your hand and repeat the oath required of every newcomer to the service, the more you can gain from the experience. I know, because I have been there.

Acknowledgments

The technical material that forms the basis of this study of military career opportunities consists entirely of official recruiting and career information published by the Department of Defense and the separate military services. In these days of huge federal budget deficits and concomitant efforts to reduce military expenditures, it seems necessary to caution that many of the programs, as well as in-service and post-service benefits, described are subject to review and change. During the preparation of the manuscript, in fact, Congress passed legislation that revised the long-standing military retirement system.

The historical and factual framework of the study, of course, is based to a large extent on unofficial materials and personal experience. Short-term changes in specific programs do not seem likely to alter the interpretive comments, opinions, and conclusions that occur throughout the book. In any case, I take full responsibility for any such statements.

Many people in and out of military service contributed to the book in a variety of ways. Although I would like to acknowledge their assistance individually, they are simply too numerous to name. I can only hope that they will accept my sincere thanks for their contributions.

Part **I**

THE MILITARY SERVICES AS MAINSTREAM AMERICA

Chapter **I**

The Role of the Military Services in the United States

Everyone loves a parade, it seems. The man next to me in the reviewing stand had become very excited as the big military band came down the avenue. A spendidly uniformed drum major strutted out in front. He wore a huge bearskin shako on his head, and he carried a shiny baton almost as long as he was tall. Behind the band marched the color guard, the massed American flags flying in the breeze. Still further behind, we could see the marching units in the colorful dress uniforms of the military services of the United States: Army, Navy, Marines, Air Force, Coast Guard.

At first all we could hear from the band was the BOOM! BOOM! of a bass drum, sounding the marching cadence. With each BOOM! the left feet of hundreds of marching men and women struck the pavement. Then, as he approached the reviewing stand, the drum major signaled to the band. The marching musicians readied their instruments. At another signal from the strutting drum major, the band struck up the stirring "Washington Post March."

We watched in admiration as each military unit passed. The men and women in the arrow-straight ranks marched proudly erect, each in perfect step with the big bass drum. As the sound of the music faded and all we could hear was the BOOM! of the drum beating out the marching cadence, my companion turned toward me.

"I have been in your country some weeks," he said, in the clipped British English of West Africa. "Only today have I seen any evidence of the military power of the United States! Why is this so?" he asked.

The man seated next to me was a senior government official from a recently independent African country. Later, we spent many hours working out answers to his question. For his question was not a simple one.

First of all, some two million men and women are serving in one or another of the military forces of the United States. Why don't we see more individuals in uniform around us? Why don't we see more military units on our streets and highways? And in our cities? In many countries around the world, we both knew, armed soldiers seem to be everywhere.

Then, we asked ourselves, who were those men and women we had watched as they marched that day? Why had we not seen them in the days before the parade? And after the parade, where had they gone? What do they do when they are not marching down the Main Streets of a thousand American cities on a patriotic holiday? Where do they fit into our society? What are their hopes and aspirations?

Perhaps you are asking yourself some of the same questions as you try to decide to what to do for the rest of your life. Or, at least, what to do after you finish school. So, perhaps a good place to start a book like this is to tell you what my friend and I concluded as a result of our long discussions.

One of the most important of our discoveries was that of the great tradition of the citizen soldier, a tradition that has had great influence on the role of the military in the United States. We have no privileged military caste in this country, nor have we ever had one.

Another factor that distinguishes the military tradition in the United States is that the armed forces are expected to serve the society from which they draw their members. And that means that they serve society in general, in peace as well as in war.

Technological advances in recent years also contribute much that helps to answer the question posed by my friend from Africa. Our military forces have not always been quick to adopt new ideas, but now they are poised at the leading edge of technology. This factor has greatly influenced the organization and disposition of our armed forces, not to mention the recruitment and training of the men and women who serve in them.

Finally, an important shift in American foreign policy, from one that emphasized a neutral role in world affairs to a policy that ranges around the globe, has greatly altered the role of the military forces of the United States since World War II. A German or a Korean, oddly enough, could be more exposed to the visible aspects of our military forces than the average American.

THE MILITARY TRADITION IN THE UNITED STATES

Your own impressions of the role of the military services of the United States have most likely been formed from watching TV shows or Hollywood movies. This is likely to be true even if you live near a major military base, despite the efforts of the armed services to reach out to the surrounding community.

Of course, there are many opportunities to see at least some of our military men and women in action. Air shows staged by the Air Force or the Navy may be seen around the nation. Perhaps you have thrilled to a mass parachute drop by airborne troopers, for example, or to a mock helicopter assault by a Marine unit. If you live near a seaport, you may even have visited a Navy ship or a Coast Guard cutter. But, even though you too may love a parade, events such as those really do not give you much of an idea about who these men and women really are or what they do most of the time.

The United States has a well-developed military tradition. Chances are that you yourself know someone who is serving in our armed forces or who has served in the recent past. Would you be surprised to learn that more than nine million Americans were in uniform during the Vietnam era, in the 1960s and 1970s? Did you know that about 1.5 million men and women serve in military reserve organizations and units, in addition to the 2.1 million or so now on active duty with the various military forces?

For the idea of the citizen soldier is the very basis of our military tradition. The citizen soldier is someone who interrupts his or her civilian life for a time to put on the uniform of one of the military services. This has often been the case during a national emergency. On the other hand, young American men and women are entering and leaving the armed forces every day, even now. After a while, whether or not there actually is a national emergency such as a war, most of these people exchange their uniform for civilian clothes and resume their individual role in American society.

Throughout our history, citizens have been expected to serve the society in which they lived. When the Pilgrims landed at Plymouth in 1620, for example, they had with them Captain Myles Standish, a professional soldier hired to help protect the tiny colony from supposedly savage Indians. Fortunately, the Indians proved to be quite friendly. So Captain Standish had little to do but train the able-bodied men of the colony in the basic arts of warfare, just in case. Other colonies followed the same pattern, and the concept of the citizen soldier became well established in the British colonies.

Each colony was required, in fact, to recruit and train its own self-defense force, or militia, from among its citizens. For perhaps the first time in history, civilians were encouraged to bear arms and participate in the defense of their community.

Many colonial militia units fought alongside regular British troops during the French and Indian Wars, for example. And some of those same colonial militiamen fired the first shots of the American Revolution, in 1775. Those "Minutemen" of Lexington and Concord, along with other militia units, then formed the core of the

Continental Army under the command of George Washington—who, not incidentally, had gained his military experience as a colonel in the Virginia militia many years earlier.

The Founding Fathers had no interest in maintaining a large standing army after independence was won, and the citizen-soldier tradition of the colonial era was institutionalized in the Constitution of the United States of America by several articles that provided for the establishment, organization, and training of militia units by the individual states.

Soon after the decisive defeat of the British at the Battle of Yorktown, in 1783, thousands of soldiers and officers simply drifted away from their Continental Army units. Most returned to their communities and farms and resumed their civilian lives. Others moved into the frontier areas, intent on carving new lives and fortunes: The land grants made to veterans of the Continental Army as reward for service during the war might be thought of as the first "GI Bill." What was left of the Continental Army was soon disbanded by Congress.

General Washington once again hung up his sword and returned to Mount Vernon to manage his plantation. But he merely exchanged the sword for the pen of the statesmen, for he soon became the wise first President of our country. George Washington, indeed, exemplifies the citizen-soldier tradition of the United States. In 1799, upon his death, Congress honored both the man and the tradition by a resolution that read in part: "To the memory of the man, first in war, first in peace, and first in the hearts of his countrymen."

Under the circumstances, the existing militias of the newly organized states took over the still important tasks of defending the frontiers of the country and maintaining internal order. In the absence of a national army, the Constitution had also provided that Congress could call upon the state militias "to execute the laws of the Union, to suppress insurrections, and repel invasions." Thus it was that the militias and the citizen soldiers they produced played important roles in the accession of Florida and expansion into Texas, for example. General Andrew Jackson, a former member of the Tennessee militia—and, otherwise, a lawyer, a judge, and a plantation owner—led a ragtag collection of militiamen and pirates to victory over superior British Army forces at New Orleans in what certainly was the strangest battle of the very strange War of 1812.

The institution of the state militias, growing out of the American colonial experience, has played an important and continuing role in the military history of the United States up to this very minute. The Army National Guard organizations in the fifty states are the direct descendants of the state militias that were recognized by the Constitution. They operate under the control of the governor of each state unless, or until, they are called into the service of the federal government by Congressional action.

In the relatively peaceful years after the Revolution, the tradition of the citizen soldier played a large role in the rapid development of the country. Moreover, service to the nation in time of peace became an important part of our military tradition.

Army officers who had no enemy to fight, for example, organized exploratory expeditions that soon spurred hundreds of thousands of Americans to seek their destinies in the West and, eventually, resulted in the expansion of the United States to the Pacific coast. The expeditions of Lewis and Clark and of John Charles Frémont, all Army officers who led Army detachments, were outstanding examples of these explorations.

For many years, every Regular Army officer who graduated from the Military Academy was trained to be a civil engineer. The basic idea was that the Army should contribute to building the new nation rather than waste time with frivolous military campaigns in the European tradition. Sylvanus Thayer, the commandant who established the engineering curriculum, later founded the Thayer School of Engineering at Dartmouth College.

The Military Academy at West Point long ago changed its curriculum, but the Army Corps of Engineers remained heavily involved in civil works. The Corps built the Panama Canal, for example. In the 1980s, Army engineers supervise the operation of inland waterways, improve harbors, and develop flood-control and other water-resource management projects all over the United States.

Under the authority of the Constitution, by which the Congress can "define and punish piracies and felonies committed on the high seas and offenses against the law of nations," the small Navy of the United States helped rid the Caribbean and Mediterranean seas of pirates, thus playing a large role in securing freedom of navigation in international waters for the merchant shipping of the world. The Navy also helped protect the lives and property of Americans stranded abroad by wars and civil disturbances, intercepted ships carrying African slaves, convoyed ships carrying former slaves to their new homes in Liberia, and contributed to the opening of new trading areas for American manufacturers and merchants.

With few battles to fight, the Navy also embarked on projects that increased our knowledge of the seven seas and the lands that border them. Exploratory expeditions, oceanographic and meteorological observations, and projects to chart the seas are all part of the Navy's contribution to peaceable navigation. In this century, Navy officers have led expeditions to explore both the North and South Poles. And the work continues.

A saying of the early nineteenth century was, "Put your trust in God, my boys, and keep your powder dry!" That advice seems to sum up this uniquely American experience in which the roles of citizen soldiers (and citizen sailors) played such an important part.

Today our modern military forces must still prepare for war, but they are also continually engaged in projects and programs designed to serve the public welfare and, at the same time, to preserve peace.

The answer to one of the questions asked by my African friend is, it seems, simple enough. If we ask where the men and women of today's military services come from, the answer is that they come from the people. And, in the best tradition of our country, they bring to the military services the hopes and dreams of the nation as a whole. In turn, the military services serve to train their members in important skills, help build character and self-discipline, and instill qualities of leadership. The tradition of the citizen soldier continues to influence American history, and the military services of the United States are today, more than ever, an integral part of American society.

CHANGING PERSPECTIVES ON WAR AND PEACE

The military services of the United States are larger and more complex than ever in our peacetime history. In general, most Americans accept this situation as a response to the threat posed by expanding Soviet military and political power, though other circumstances have recently been influential.

Shortly after the end of World War II, the United States led the world by embarking on a global foreign policy dedicated at first to blocking the further expansion of the Soviet Union into Europe. Soon, a consequence of that policy extended the influence of the United States into Asia, Africa, and Latin America. Armed forces were organized, or reorganized, to support the new policy moves. To a large extent, this policy of "containment" depended on the superiority that the United States enjoyed because of its monopoly of nuclear weapons. Before long, however, the Soviet Union was able to develop its own nuclear weapons; the monopoly of the United States no longer exists.

These events have directly influenced the recent development of the military forces of the United States. First, the need to support our global foreign policy means that a large portion of our armed forces is located outside the continental United States. Second, the military forces have invested a great deal of energy and money in an effort to gain and hold a technological advantage over the Soviet Union.

As a nation dedicated to peace, the United States cannot afford the luxury of the military establishment required to match the huge, heavily armed military forces of the Soviet Union. Instead, its emphasis has been on building relatively small, highly trained, and mobile military forces that can deter or defeat a potential enemy because of their technological superiority, whether on land, at sea, or in the air.

You may begin to see that these developments have a great influence on the recruitment, training, and assignment of men and women to and within our military services. How can this affect you? Well, most of the developments in the high-tech fields being explored by the military services have both military and civilian applications. Specialists in a military occupation may move back and forth between the military services and the civilian economy with considerable ease during their careers. Let's look at a few examples.

The United States Air Force and the aviation units of the Navy, the Marine Corps, and even the Army benefited enormously from the development of the jet aircraft engine. Yet perhaps the most important result has been the worldwide revolution in civil aviation that the jet engines brought about. Well-trained military pilots and jet engine mechanics are often able to find employment with commercial airlines after they have completed their military service.

While the American decision to rely on nuclear weapons as the foundation of our military power has been controversial, no nuclear weapons have been used in actual warfare since 1945. The nuclear technology developed for, or by, the military has instead been applied to the production of energy: energy needed to drive the Navy's capital ships, for example. In the civilian sector, the focus has been on the development of nuclear power plants, which already supply about twenty percent of the country's energy and promise an even greater contribution as supplies of petroleum and other fossil fuels become scarcer and more expensive. Nuclear technicians trained in the military should be able to find civilian employment with only minor retraining.

Less spectacular, but very important, is the military's use of sophisticated electronics in the performance of many military tasks. Personnel, financial, and supply records are all maintained on computers. Many other applications of computers and other advanced electronics equipment are common in today's armed forces, often right down to the combat units facing an enemy. Many electronics systems now in use by the military services were first developed for civilian use; radios, television, and computers are examples. However, it is also the case that electronic devices and systems first developed for the military, such as radar and sonar devices, have been adapted for nonmilitary uses. You can draw your own conclusions about the career benefits that you might gain from the technical training that the military can offer you. Are you interested in robotics, for example? So are the military services.

WHAT THE MILITARY SERVICES CAN OFFER YOU

The time has long since passed when the members of the military services were mostly foot-slogging infantrymen, dashing cavalrymen, and swashbuckling sailors. The vast majority of the men and women serving in the five military forces will never face an enemy; those who do are likely to be highly skilled technicians. Every infantry soldier has at his disposal a whole range of advanced weapons and equipment to make him more effective, and for every rifleman in an infantry squad the Army has dozens of other soldiers who provide essential support services to that squad. The dashing horse cavalrymen of history have been replaced by tank drivers and gunners who must be able to operate sophisticated electronic equipment. Most of the men and women in today's Navy will never serve on a fighting ship, though their jobs are very necessary to the success of those who do. Only a few members of the Air Force actually fly those screaming jets; in fact, only a relatively few men and women in the Air Force fly at all except as passengers.

What do they do? The military services have, between them, more than two thousand job specialties. Most of them fall under the one hundred or so broad clusters of "military occupations" that are equivalent or closely related to civilian occupations. Many of those occupations are about as old as civilization itself: cooks and bakers, barbers, and clerks, for example. Many others are at the leading edge of high technology: pilots of supersonic jets, computer programmers, electronic repairers, and nuclear energy specialists, to name a few. Whatever your job or career interests, one or another of the military services can probably match them. We shall discuss more about how the military job pie is cut up in Chapter III, "The Military Services as a Work Force."

Right now, it seems more important to point out that you do not have to be either lucky or a technological wizard to take advantage of this situation. All the military services recruit new members on a voluntary basis. As a volunteer, you have quite a bit to say about what you want to do once you join the military.

Also important is the fact that all the military services offer young women greatly increased employment and career opportunities. More than two hundred thousand American women serve in the five uniformed military services. Many are performing jobs that were once restricted to men. Women fly military airplanes, they command Coast Guard vessels and Army support units, and they carry out essential jobs in most of the hundreds of military occupational specialties in the various services. The only real restriction women face is that they cannot be assigned to jobs that could expose them to active combat.

The technological environment of our modern military services also means that its members must be highly trained and educated. A very important consideration, however, is that the military services themselves provide the necessary training in most cases. In fact, the five military services together operate the largest vocational training establishment in the United States. You don't need to have any civilian experience to land a good job in the military services. But, beyond the vocational training they provide, the services offer exceptional opportunities for advanced education, up to the doctoral level in some cases. We shall explore some of these programs for both technical training and general education elsewhere in this book, particularly in Chapter IV, "Educational Opportunities in the Military Services."

Those who look forward to the excitement and rigors of a traditional military career will, of course, find many opportunities awaiting them. Despite recent emphasis on nuclear weapons, military planners have not overlooked the need for strong, well-trained, highly skilled conventional forces for rapid movement almost anywhere in the world. Such combat forces emphasize the traditional fighting arms—infantry, artillery, and armor—along with the Air Force and Navy personnel and units necessary to move and support those forces in any potential battle zone. Those forces include the airborne units, the Army Rangers, and Special Forces personnel trained to operate behind enemy lines.

The global responsibilities assigned to the various military forces also take into consideration the possible future need to expand the total active-duty force or, perhaps, to augment a part of it. The primary sources of trained personnel are the various military reserve forces. Each of the "regular" military services has a reserve component organized, equipped, and trained for such a situation; these include the state Army and Air Force National Guard organizations, but they are governed by laws that restrict availability to national emergencies.

Everyone who serves in the military forces may be subject to service in the reserves, especially first-term enlisted men and women who decide not to continue their military career. However, many men and women have built substantial careers in the reserve forces as citizen soldiers, with no significant interruption to their civilian careers. Some of the alternatives to a career in the active military forces are discussed in Chapter XI, "You and the Reserve Forces."

Chapter **II**

Getting Started in the Military

Recruiters for the military services of the United States at times appear to be falling all over themselves in their efforts to enroll young men and women. The principal inducements include the promise of well-paying jobs with no experience necessary; free training, with full pay, in hundreds of specialized fields; opportunities for advanced education at little or no cost; and prospects of a rewarding career, with regular promotions, in just about any occupational field you can imagine. A Navy recruiter recently told me, with only a hint of a smile, that the Navy offered every job known to man except two: farmer and rancher. There is much to be said for this approach, though the very term "military service" seems to suggest that something more than a mere job is involved.

The rewards of military service are considerable. Besides their pay, members of the military services receive free clothing, meals, and housing (officers must pay); free medical and dental care (and unlimited sick leave with pay); extra pay for certain assignments or kinds of duty; bonuses for enlistment or reenlistment in some jobs; and thirty days' paid vacation every year. Military personnel and their dependents also enjoy discount supermarkets and department stores and access to a variety of low-cost recreational facilities. Add to this the possibility of retirement after only twenty years' service, and you have what business recruiters call a great benefits package. Is there a catch? Well, yes and no. In this chapter we shall look more closely at the benefits package.

We have seen that an important goal of military planners is to gain and hold technological superiority over any potential enemy. Behind this idea is the belief that smaller numbers of well-trained, highly skilled military personnel will be able to defeat a large, less technologically advanced enemy force. Therefore, every member of any military unit in the armed forces of the United States must be highly skilled in his or her specialization. Moreover, each must also be highly motivated and self-disciplined. Obviously, not everyone can meet those qualifications. What does it take to start a military career? What does it take to stay in a military career?

HOW YOU CAN QUALIFY FOR A MILITARY CAREER

First of all, the military services require educated men and women between seventeen and thirty-five years of age who are physically fit. Age limits vary between services.

All applicants are screened to make sure that they do not have criminal records. Psychological evaluation and drug screening are included in the physical examination given to every applicant.

Most military services permit married applicants to enlist, but terms and conditions vary.

The minimum educational requirement for enlistment in any of the military services is a high school diploma or its equivalent. If you are thinking about dropping out of school to enlist in the Marines, for example, you had better think again. Ninety-three percent of the men and women who entered the military services in 1984 had high school diplomas. All five services have delayed-entry programs that permit you to enlist, sometimes for a specific military occupational specialty (or MOS), but to stay in school until you have qualified for a diploma. If you are already in college, the services also have delayed-entry programs (called DEP) for prospective enlisted recruits and officer candidates.

In your own best interests, therefore, you should start investigating career opportunities in the military services as early as possible, certainly no later than the fall of your senior year in high school. An early start affords you a wider choice of programs and occupational specialties. If you find something especially attractive, you can enlist under a deferred-entry program and begin your active military service after graduation from high school. Meanwhile, you will be assigned to an inactive reserve organization. Active service under the terms of your enlistment may be delayed for as much as a year. Start even earlier, during your junior year, if you are interested in an appointment to one of the service academies.

Completion of high school is not the only objective. Rather, graduation from high school indicates that you have a better chance of completing the initial technical schooling that usually follows basic military training. Moreover, it helps recruiters to judge your potential for later advanced training in your specialization and eventual promotion to more responsible military assignments.

Whatever you do, don't succumb to the "senior syndrome" and think that you can coast through your final year in high school. Instead, you should work at improving your study skills and aim for the best grades you can get, especially in the hard subjects like science and mathematics. Joining a military service is not the way to escape from the classroom, as we shall see later.

Nor is a high school diploma all you may need. The services are interested in young people who have taken part in some extracurricular activity: team sports, school clubs, Scouting, the Sea Cadets, or service organizations like 4-H clubs. You may get even a better reception at the recruiting office if you were a team captain, an officer in student government, or an Eagle Scout. Those accomplishments suggest leadership potential, and the military services are looking for leaders. Furthermore, your participation in extracurricular activities can confirm the high level of self-discipline needed in a military career.

Early in the recruiting process, you are given a test to determine whether you meet the service's requirements. If you did not complete high school, your score on this test is especially important. It may be possible to enter one of the armed services without finishing high school, but those who lack diplomas may find that their choices of assignment and potential for training and advancement are limited.

So far we have been talking about how you can qualify for enlistment in one of the military services. In general, minimum qualification starts you with the lowest enlisted rating, E-1: a private in the Army or Marines, a seaman recruit in the Navy or Coast Guard, an airman basic in the Air Force.

All services offer opportunities to enlist in a grade higher than E-1. Generally, however, you must have had either some education beyond high school or experience in a specialty that is badly needed by the service.

The Army, for example, offers a grade up to E-4 to some graduates of two-year community colleges or technical schools who enlist for at least two years. By the end of your enlistment, if you plan ahead, you should have accumulated enough money under the New GI Bill to permit you to return to college to complete a four-year degree program. This and similar programs of other services are discussed in Chapter IV.

Members of the Civil Air Patrol and the Sea Cadets and graduates of the Junior Reserve Officers Training program (JROTC) may also be awarded a higher entry grade upon enlistment, up to E-3.

If you want to jump over the enlistment process and become an officer, you should plan to complete four years of college, at least. The services acquire commissioned officers in four ways:

1. Graduation from one of the national military academies: West Point (Army), Annapolis (Navy, Marines), the Air Force Academy, or the Coast Guard Academy. If qualified, you may be able to secure an appointment and enter from high school, from

college, or from enlisted status (either active duty or reserve). Appointments are highly competitive. (See Chapter IV.)
2. Completion of the senior Reserve Officers Training Program (Army, Navy, Air Force) at an accredited college or university. Scholarships are available (see Chapter IV). Most Naval ROTC programs offer graduates the opportunity for a commission in the Marine Corps.
3. Successful completion of an Officer Training Program, usually after graduation from a four-year college or university. Attendance at an Officer Training Program may also be possible for well-qualified enlisted men and women who have not completed college.
4. Direct appointment. Usually limited to graduates of professional schools (medical and dental schools, nursing schools, law schools, schools of theology, etc.) and to professionals who have acquired experience or skills in fields in demand by the services. Men and women in these categories are often awarded military commissions at ranks above entry level.

APPROACHES TO CAREER PLANNING

Your choice of service depends to some extent upon your own interests and qualifications. In other respects, the choice may be highly personal or entirely subjective. A few considerations that might influence your choice are suggested below.

First, all military services are specialized work forces. In the United States, they are unique because they are also organized to provide varied, often complex, education and training to their members. The recruitment procedures for the services are basically similar because all are looking for men and women who can benefit from this training and then go on to do a job that the service needs done. Retention in service and advancement in rank and pay depend as much upon achievement of specified levels of military training and education as on job performance.

Therefore, though each service has its own distinctive customs, traditions, and uniforms, they share common enlistment policies and goals. The wide variety of enlistment and officer procurement programs within these general policies can be, on the other hand, somewhat bewildering. Some of the variety is caused by differences in requirements among the services, but much of it is precisely because the services are all looking for the same kind of person.

This means that you are in a seller's market and you are the seller. If you are otherwise qualified, you can probably have your choice of some excellent programs. In the end, however, you may have to do some shopping. Varying conditions encourage the development of new enlistment programs and the withdrawal of others.

Second, when you join any military service, you do so for a period of eight years. Part of that time, varying from two to six years, is spent on active duty, the remainder in some reserve status. For example, the Army offers two-year enlistments: You serve two years on active duty and six years in the Army Reserve. Other services offer enlistment from three to six years but always with some reserve obligation unless you reenlist.

Now, two years in the Army may be just what you need to take advantage of the New GI Bill, accumulate money to enroll in a business administration course, and prepare yourself for a civilian career as a stockbroker.

On the other hand, the shorter the tour of active duty, the less choice you have among the training and job opportunities the services offer. Why should they spend time and money training an enlistee for a highly technical job when he or she will be leaving the service before becoming productive? As the extreme example, the Navy offers the best enlisted career opportunities to those who enlist for six years and also generous reenlistment bonuses at the end of that period. Obviously, the Navy wants you for a long time, and that is fine so long as you understand what is involved, you are fully qualified, and you are willing to work hard for a Navy career.

So, if you enlist in the Army for two years with the objective of acquiring college funds, you probably shouldn't expect a very challenging job after basic training. Still, as we shall see, you can probably parlay the two years into a commission as an Army officer at a later time. You could, for example, enroll in a college or university that offers Army ROTC training and skip the ROTC basic program.

We do not have enough space in this chapter to explore all the programs and career opportunities offered by the military services. Suffice it to say that the key consideration in any career planning is to have some idea of what you want to do with your life. If you haven't yet developed a general objective, the military services offer many fine career programs to those who are qualified and willing to work hard.

AT THE RECRUITING STATION

There are many steps to enlisting in any of the military services in these days of all-volunteer forces. A visit to a recruiting station is only the first step, but an essential one. There, representatives of one of the services, can give you basic information about life in military service, current rates of pay, and other benefits of a military career. The recruiter cannot promise you a specific job, but he or she can counsel you about qualifications and assist you with the processing that can result in an offer of a training program leading to a job in the service of your choice.

During your first visit to a recruiting office, you can expect to be interviewed by a recruiter to determine whether you have the necessary qualifications for that service. A good idea, therefore, is to call in advance for an appointment. You will be asked about your educational background, your hobbies and other interests, your participation in sports and other extracurricular activities. You may be asked what you want to be doing in ten years. If you haven't given that much thought, perhaps you had better do so.

The recruiter will also ask you some personal questions: your marital status, for example, and your medical history (childhood diseases, surgical operations, broken bones, eye problems, allergies, possible physical defects). He or she will ask if you have a police record and if you have used drugs such as marijuana or cocaine.

This is a preliminary interview, but you should be completely honest with the recruiter. Misinformation, or concealing information, may prevent further processing. You, of course, can also ask questions of the recruiter. After the interview, provided you want to continue the processing and the recruiter feels that you are qualified, the recruiter will probably set a date for a second visit. If you are under eighteen years of age, you may be asked to bring one or both parents with you at that time.

Further recruit processing varies among the services, but you can expect to complete some or all of the following:

1. Enlistment screening test, mostly math and English usage, to provide further information about your knowledge and ability to fit into a service occupation or job.
2. Medical prescreening form, to provide medical background to the doctors who later conduct your physical examination.
3. Preenlistment forms, to provide personal information—where you live, your parents, your social security status, and so on. One of these forms will ask about drugs; another will authorize a check of police records.
4. Practice test for the Armed Services Vocational Aptitude Battery (ASVAB) if you have not already taken the test at your high school or elsewhere. The practice test will familiarize you

with the ASVAB, which is the basic enlistment qualification test. It will also give you and the recruiter an idea of how you might score on the test, or where you may need additional study.
5. An orientation movie or videotape, with scenes from service life.
6. A job-interest interview, during which the recruiter will review with you what you have done so far and tell you whether you appear to meet the basic qualifications for enlistment in that service.

If you do meet the qualifications for enlistment, the recruiter will schedule your official ASVAB test at a nearby testing station or send you directly to a Military Entrance Processing Station (MEPS). You may also be told to bring certain papers with you on your next visit to the recruiting station: an official birth certificate, any medical records requested by the recruiter, your high school diploma or GED certificate, your Social Security card, two other pieces of personal identification, and, if applicable, your marriage certificate, divorce papers, or citizenship papers.

THE ARMED SERVICES VOCATIONAL APTITUDE BATTERY

Enlisted men and women can often select their career field or military specialization during the recruiting process. Much depends on the scores attained on the ASVAB. Each service has established minimum qualifying scores for various parts of the test. The score you make on a particular vocational profile helps to determine whether you are qualified for training and specialization in that vocational group. If you fail to make an acceptable score on one or more parts of the test, you may be disqualified for enlistment.

The ASVAB is an objective or multiple-choice test that helps evaluate your general academic ability, your English and math skills, and your aptitude in four vocational fields: mechanical arts and crafts, business and clerical skills, electronics and electrical trades, and a general field called health, social, and technology.

The test comprises more than three hundred questions under ten subject titles as shown in the table. Each part of the test is timed; a total of about two and one half hours is allowed to complete the entire test. Answers to questions are recorded on a separate sheet.

Part	Subject	Number of Questions	Minutes Allowed
1.	General Science	25	11
2.	Arithmetic Reasoning	30	36
3.	Word Knowledge	35	11
4.	Paragraph Comprehension	15	13
5.	Numerical Operations	50	3
6.	Coding Speed	84	7
7.	Auto and Shop Information	25	11
8.	Mathematics Knowledge	25	24
9.	Mechanical Comprehension	25	19
10.	Electronics Information	20	9
	TOTALS	334	2 hours, 24 minutes

The Armed Services Vocational Aptitude Battery

If you are not familiar with this kind of test, you may be able to purchase a practice manual before you take the ASVAB. You may also be able to take the test before you ever visit a recruiter. The ASVAB is given periodically at many high schools and some community colleges and technical schools. Your guidance or career counselor should be able to tell you when and where. Scores achieved on the ASVAB are valid for about two years. However, you may have to take the test again during your enlistment processing.

Your scores on the ASVAB are used to see what types of jobs you are best suited for in the military service of your choice. They may also be used to help determine your eligibility for training at military and civilian schools, for enlisted educational and advancement programs, and for programs that lead to commissioning as an officer. You can take the ASVAB after you enlist, but scores may vary each time you take the test; in some cases people score worse on repeat tests.

After you have received your ASVAB scores, assuming that they are pretty good, your recruiter may discuss possible training and job options with you. However, the recruiter may not offer jobs. The final determination of your eligibility for any training program or career field is made at the Military Entrance Processing Station, and then only after all the other results are in.

WHAT TO EXPECT IN MILITARY SERVICE

Military service, like most civilian professional fields, is hierar-chical in nature. That is, your duties, responsibilities, and privileges depend upon where you stand on the career ladder. On the other hand, the military services are rich in tradition and are more likely to emphasize service and "mission" than are civilian professions.

When you are sworn in at the Military Entrance Processing Station you agree to dedicate yourself to the service of your country and to defend it against all enemies, foreign and domestic. Early in your training, you will be reminded in various ways that you are identified with and part of a unit, an organization, or a service with lofty goals and objectives that take precedence over individual aspirations.

At the same time, the services place great emphasis on the development of individual initiative. This situation, however, has certain rules. The basic rule is that the exercise of individual initiative must work to benefit the "mission" or task of your unit or organization. Heroes in military tradition are honored less for their individual actions on the battlefield than for the fact that what they did contributed to the success of the mission of their unit. It is for this reason, incidentally, that the services seek young people who already demonstrate self-discipline and the ability to identify with the goals of the group.

In passing, it may be worth noting that the concern of the military services about drug and alcohol abuse is related to the same idea. The use of drugs and alcohol may be disastrous to the unit and its mission simply because their effects are to muddle minds and cause unpredictable behavior.

Let us assume that you have already talked to a recruiter in the service of your choice. He or she has checked your ASVAB scores and high school credentials and discussed with you a delayed-entry program so that you can finish high school. There seemed to be no health problems, and the recruiter scheduled you for a medical examination at an MEPS.

You passed the physical and did well on the aptitude test. A military career information specialist has discussed several training options with you, and you have chosen one. What is the next step?

Once you have made the decision to enlist, an enlistment contract is drawn up. The contract specifies the enlistment program, the enlistment date (immediate or deferred), and other options. You now take the enlistment oath, but you return home under the deferred-entry program until you graduate from high school. Until you reach the predetermined enlistment date, you are assigned to the appropriate reserve force on inactive status.

It is important to understand that you have entered into a contract that binds both you and the service you chose. If for some reason the service cannot fit you into your guaranteed training program when it is scheduled, you are no longer bound by the contract. You do, however, have three alternatives: (1) select another date for the same training; (2) choose another specialty, along with a new starting date; or (3) decide not to join the service. On the other hand, don't forget that the contract also binds you. If the service keeps its bargain, you must carry out your part of the contract.

Let's say that everything worked out the way it was supposed to, and you were sent to a training center to start your basic training. What then?

Recruit training is designed to orient new enlisted members to the military. It may last from six to ten weeks, depending upon the service and the prospective military specialty. According to one official publication, "Through basic training, recruits gain the pride, knowledge, discipline, and physical conditioning necessary to serve as members of the Army, Navy, Air Force, Marine Corps, and Coast Guard."

That reads very well, but you should know that basic training can be a rugged, personally demanding experience. You are issued uniforms and thrown in with a group of forty or so strangers. Your days are long, filled with classes, physical conditioning, and field exercises, with little free time. For most recruits, happiness is completing basic training!

When you have completed basic training—and not everyone does—the specialization you chose (or were offered) when you entered military service will determine your assignments and your eligibility for promotion during your service career. That is why you must choose carefully from among the available specialties.

The military occupations discussed in Chapter III and listed in Appendix C include the broad fields of administration, health services, personnel management, communications, public affairs, police work, electronics, mechanical trades, and many others, including the combat specialties (infantry, artillery, and armor). An important consideration for recruits may be to select a military specialization that has a civilian counterpart.

Once you have completed the first phases of training, you will increasingly experience the satisfactions of military service and, of course, the many advantages. One of the benefits highly valued by many former service men and women is the opportunity to meet people from all over the country and from all walks of life. In recent years, important changes in the military services have helped ensure that they reflect, to the extent possible, the social fabric of the country.

Not everyone who enters military service chooses to complete a full career of twenty or thirty years. In fact, only about fifteen percent of those who join the services remain long enough to qualify for retirement.

Those who decide not to remain in the active armed forces may, however, qualify for substantial benefits. Almost anyone who chooses well can leave the service with special skills and experience that will qualify him or her for a rewarding civilian career. All-service programs even offer the opportunity to accumulate sufficient money to finance a college education. In addition, first-term enlistees also have an obligation to remain in the reserves and an opportunity to follow an income-producing quasi-military career. And, of course, many other valuable benefits are available to honorably discharged veterans.

For those who elect to complete a military career, the benefits may be even more substantial. Almost all military personnel can find opportunities for further education, up to the doctoral level. Enlisted personnel may receive reenlistment bonuses that can add substantial savings over the years. All the military services are giving considerable emphasis to the "military family," from day-care centers for the children of working couples to special joint assignments when both parents are military members. Both officers and enlisted members of the armed forces are engaged in the activities and programs of professional societies and associations. Many are involved in community public-service programs and organizations: Scouting, for example. And, finally, the benefits that come with military retirement include every benefit of active service plus a few more such as space-available travel on military passenger aircraft and the whole range of veterans' benefits.

As in any career, of course, you will get out of your career in military service what you put into it—and, it seems, a bit more. The military profession still demands a little more dedication to service-beyond-self, some occasional hardships, and unexpected separations from family and loved ones. On the other side of the ledger are the satisfactions that come from service to the nation, specialized training in many fields that can prepare you for a rewarding civilian occupation, opportunities for advanced education, and other worthwhile compensations. The choice is yours, but there probably has never been a better time to consider making a career for yourself in the military service of the United States.

Chapter **III**

The Military Services as a Work Force

The five military services employ the largest work force in the United States. About 2.1 million men and women serve in the uniformed services; another million or so are full-time civilian employees.

The United States Army is the largest of the military services, with about 780,000 members in uniform, followed by the Air Force, with more than 600,000 members. The Navy accounts for 565,000 men and women; and its land forces, the Marine Corps, add about 200,000 more to the total naval force. The smallest of the military services is the United States Coast Guard, with approximately 37,000 officers and enlisted men and women.

What all these military services have in common is the mission to defend the United States, its institutions, and its interests, whether at home or abroad. Each service has a role to play in fulfilling this mission. But all have one important characteristic in common: Each service is organized so that it can operate autonomously, regardless of the geographical setting or the civilian society in which it may find itself while carrying out assigned tasks.

If you think about this fact for a moment, you will recognize its importance to anyone who is considering a military career. For just about any job or occupational field that you can imagine can be found in one or another of the military services. Obviously, the reverse of that statement is also true: Many of the jobs available in the armed services are equivalent to, or closely related to, occupational and career fields found in the civilian work force.

As has been said, only a small portion of the 2.1 million people in military service will ever engage an enemy in combat. Only about one of every seven enlisted members of the Army and Marine Corps is classified as an infantryman or a tank crewman. The other six are working at jobs that support the men who do the fighting. Of course, many of these people will be right on the battlefield, in very close support indeed. Many others will be handling supplies, providing transportation, maintaining equipment, and operating communica-

24

tions facilities, data processing centers, or hospitals, for example. So, let's see how this all works out for the military services as a group.

The chart shows how approximately 1.8 million military jobs are divided among enlisted men and women in the armed forces. In this chapter we shall look only at the enlisted military specialties, which include about eighty-five percent of the jobs in the armed services. Commissioned officers are not usually thought of as "specialists," but as leaders and managers.

In this chart you can quickly see how the pie is divided. Look first at the Combat Specialties, which include the infantrymen and tank crewmen mentioned earlier plus artillery crewmen, combat engineers, and members of Special Forces units. You can see that those 221,500 jobs account for about thirteen percent of all positions filled by the enlisted personnel of the five military services.

Many more of the jobs are in such categories as Administrative (355,000 jobs, held by 20.4 percent of enlisted personnel), Vehicle and Machinery Mechanic (about 258,600, or 14.9 percent of the jobs), and Electronic and Electrical Equipment Repair (about 253,200 jobs, on 14.6 percent of enlisted personnel). The thousands of jobs in such fields as Transportation and Material Handling; Engineering, Science, and Technical; and Health Care reflect the fact that the military services much be prepared to do almost anything, anywhere. Other military jobs are found in such fields as Media and Public Affairs, Construction, and the Machine Trades.

All this should help answer another of the questions that my African friend and I asked ourselves after that parade: What do those hundreds of marching men and women in uniform do when they are not "on parade"? The answer is that they are working at a job, or getting ready to go to work, or relaxing after work, or perhaps enjoying a well-earned vacation from work.

Like most American workers, the men and women of the military services have well-defined jobs, complete with "job descriptions," and enjoy more or less established, career-related life-styles. Despite similarities between the military and civilian work forces, however, no one pretends that differences do not exist. In the next section, we discuss similarities. Later we shall examine some aspects of military service that set it apart from the civilian work force.

SIMILARITIES BETWEEN MILITARY AND CIVILIAN WORK FORCES

In a way, life in the military services resembles that of a firefighter in a municipal fire department. The firefighter spends a great deal of

Distribution of Enlisted Personnel
by Occupational Cluster

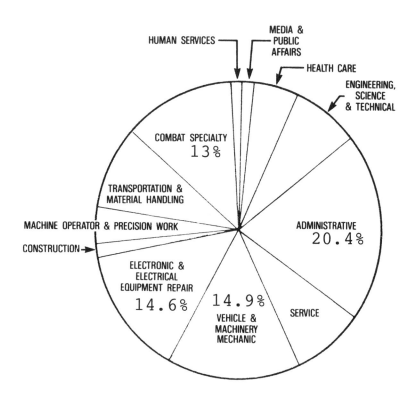

time and energy preparing for the big fire that may never come. When, or if, the alarm sounds, he has to be ready to move rapidly, apply the necessary means to put out the fire, and take other actions to prevent it from spreading and thus endangering the whole neighborhood.

The firefighter must study and train constantly to maintain and improve his knowledge and skills. He must always be sure that all the firefighting equipment, his own and that of his station, is in the best possible condition for any emergency. In his free time, he is probably preparing for the promotion examination for the next higher firefighting rank. If everything else is taken care of, he may sit around playing cards with other members of his crew, or he may help with a station project: collecting toys for neighborhood kids at Christmas, conducting schoolchildren on a tour of the firehouse, or selling tickets for the annual Firemen's Ball!

Not every civilian wants to be a firefighter, but we are all grateful that some do. On the other hand, many civilians work in service occupations that are carried on twenty-four hours a day: airline pilots, bus drivers, railroaders, and truckers, perhaps. Workers in hospitals, hotels, food service establishments, and the communications industry are other examples. Many others, of course, work while most of us sleep: the people who edit, publish, and distribute our morning newspapers in time for breakfast, for instance. Industrial plants may operate around the clock. More and more data-processing centers work all night so that those who need the data can have it in usable form when they come to work during what we still like to call "normal working hours."

Employment and employment conditions in the military services resemble those in the civilian work force in many ways. We might compare the combat-ready forces, including the Army and Marine Corps tactical divisions and the Air Force, Navy, and Marine units that support them, to the municipal fire department. Other responsibilities in strategic areas require many military units to be operational twenty-four hours a day. Units of this kind may be found in the North American Air Defense Command (NORAD), the Strategic Air Command (SAC), among radio monitoring units and agencies, and among the worldwide military communications facilities.

But the military services must also carry out many of the same kinds of administrative and other support activities that we know in civilian life. They move large quantities of supplies and military equipment and thousands of military passengers around the United States and, indeed, around the globe. They operate storage depots, vehicle and equipment maintenance shops, clinics and hospitals, sports and recreation facilities and programs, and data-processing centers. They feed two million men and women every day, plan and supervise the production of military equipment and weapons, publish newspapers and magazines, operate radio and TV stations, and provide community services. They may even design, build, and maintain buildings, roads and bridges, airfields, railroads, canals, and dams. What, then makes the military services different?

SPECIAL FEATURES OF THE MILITARY WORK FORCE

Uniforms, you may say, set the military services apart. Of course, that is true. Nor does it matter that millions of people in the civilian work force wear uniforms. You can probably think of quite a few: policemen and security guards, gas station attendants, firemen, post office workers, bus drivers, nurses, waiters and waitresses, airline employees, mechanics, and baseball players, among others. Uniforms help us identify certain kinds of civilian workers. In most cases, however, civilian uniforms are special forms of work clothing. Military uniforms are somewhat different.

Military uniforms do, of course, serve to identify members of the armed forces. Traditionally, the right to wear the uniform of one of the military services is governed by laws, both national and international. In time of war or in a zone of military action, recognized military uniforms distinguish the "combatants" from civilians, although this fact may seem to be ignored in some parts of the world these days. In the United States, the Supreme Court recognizes that men and women in the uniforms of the military services are a separate community within the population, subject to separate laws, regulations, and customs.

Further, however, military uniforms have symbolic meaning. "Service" is the key word. Wearing the uniform is evidence that you have dedicated yourself to the service of your nation, in time of peace as well as in time of war. Those who enter one of the armed forces are expected to identify themselves with the goals and missions of that particular service, even if it means subordinating their personal goals and objectives. In the logical extreme, the symbolism of the uniform is that you are prepared to sacrifice your life for your country.

In the workaday world of peacetime military service, however, the primary effect is more likely to be that you are expected to endure some inconvenience or, rarely, make a real personal sacrifice "for the good of the service." No union representatives can intervene, for example, when you have to work overtime, Sundays, or holidays with no extra pay. After you have completed your initial training and are settled into a job that you like, you may find yourself called away for a surprise inspection, some refresher military training, a practice parade, or a work detail unrelated to your job assignment. Annoying, but not fatal. Maybe you will miss a movie you planned to see because you have to go back to the office to catch up with paperwork or whatever.

Even in peacetime, however, you may be called upon for personal sacrifice. If you are in a combat unit, for example, you may be involved in distant maneuvers that can severely limit your social life (or, perhaps, your family life). Navy, Marine, or Coast Guard personnel may be subject to long tours of sea duty. Mercy missions and disaster relief projects may be initiated on short notice and may involve large numbers of men and women on twenty-four-hour-a-day schedules for extended periods.

So, once you become a member of a military service, you may find that the "good of the service" often comes ahead of your own needs and desires. The order of priority may seem to be reversed at first, but most recruits adapt quickly. In both the short run and the long term, a military career offers many rewards and compensations in return for service. Indeed, for those who have "the right stuff," it can offer extraordinary opportunities for personal advancement and professional achievement. Department of Defense statistics support that statement. In recent years more than half the first-term enlisted men and women have reenlisted. The reenlistment rate for career enlisted members of the five military services has been much greater: eighty-five percent.

Just as in the civilian world of work, the military services pay their employees to do a job. What is different is that the services do not require any previous experience. What other employer will pay you a full salary while you are being trained for a job?

You may have heard that pay in the military services lags behind that of civilian workers. Keep in mind that most of your first year—or more—of service may be spent as a trainee, with full pay. In a relatively short time you will probably find that your pay and allowances (for uniforms, meals, housing, and so on), plus such things as free medical and dental care, discount prices in military stores (the commissaries and post exchanges), thirty-day paid vacation each year, and income tax advantages—not to mention tuition-free technical training—have probably put you ahead of civilian counterparts in total income.

Moreover, even without experience, qualified high school graduates may be able to enlist in certain training programs that provide a significant pay advantage. Not only is the starting pay higher; chances for rapid promotion are also excellent.

Most Navy recruits, for example, enter service with the rank of seaman recruit, in the lowest pay grade, E-1. A Navy training program in advanced electronics can bring in qualified recruits with the rating of seaman, in pay grade E-3. Following successful completion of the inital technical training, the trainee may be promoted to petty officer third class (E-4). At this point, he or she is being paid at the rate of about $14,500 a year. Not bad going for someone just out of high school who is still a full-time student.

At this point, you may be somewhat confused by military terms. Let's take a moment to try to clarify the situation. To start with, all the military services use the same pay scale for enlisted members. The scale begins with the lowest pay grade, E-1, and goes up to E-9. On the other hand, not all the services use the same titles or ranks for people in those pay grades. An E-3 in the Navy or Coast Guard is called a seaman; but an E-3 in the Marine Corps, which is really part of the Navy, is known as a lance corporal. In the Army, an E-3 is a private first class; the equivalent Air Force rank is airman first class. The non-commissioned officer ranks generally begin with pay grade E-4, but not every E-4 is a non-commissioned officer.

The accompanying illustrations show the ranks and titles used by the five military services, arranged by pay grade. Appendix A contains information on enlisted pay and allowances; Appendix B for officers. Pay scales are usually adjusted upward each year for increases in the cost of living. In recent years such adjustments have added about three percent each year to basic pay.

Also note that military pay increases for each year of service. These increases are known as longevity steps. In other words, the longer you serve in a particular pay grade, the more money you earn. Appendices A and B also show some of the allowances paid certain categories of enlisted men and women. Allowances are not considered part of military basic pay and have traditionally been considered as tax-free income. (The Navy pay figures in the example used above include both pay and allowances.)

Each military service has developed other enlistment options that permit recruits to enter in an advanced pay grade. Otherwise qualified high school graduates who complete the Junior Reserve Officers Training Program (JROTC) may enter service with a pay grade up to E-3. A student who has already earned a two-year college degree may be able to join the Army with the rank of E-3, under the Accelerated Promotion for Education Program. After one year of satisfactory service, he or she may be eligible for promotion to E-4. You should consult a local recruiter for similar programs that match your qualifications and interests.

As we have seen, the military services are generally willing and able to pay their members well for performance on the job. But you should also know that there is not much room in the services for those who do not produce. In the armed forces, the rule of thumb is "Get promoted or get out!" You may not hear the phrase from a recruiter, but that is what is implied by such current slogans as "Army! Be All You Can Be!" The Air Force expects you to "Aim High." These are more than mere words. Living longer does not ensure anyone a promotion in these days of the all-volunteer military services, if it ever did.

Your promotion potential is estimated before you enter military service. If you cannot make the grade, either as a trainee or, later, in the job to which you are assigned, you may be in trouble with both your career and yourself. An important difference between the civilian work force and military service is that once you have enlisted you have assumed a contractual obligation that is enforceable under law. You cannot just decide that you will drop out of a training program or, later, walk off your assigned job without incurring a penalty.

On the other hand, if you are not meeting the standards set by the service, you can be released involuntarily from a training program and reassigned. If, after you have completed your initial training, you are not performing well in your assigned job, you may also be reassigned.

Earlier we said that the military services are hierarchical organizations. Where you stand on the career ladder has a great influence upon your status in life, as well as on the extent of your privileges. The hierarchy of bosses runs up the line from you to the commander of your service, who is usually called chief of staff because even he has a boss. In this case, the "boss" is the President of the United States, who is commander in chief of all the U.S. armed services. The hierarchy of bosses in the military services is called the chain of command, and the relationships that it suggests may also be enforced under the laws of the United States.

When you take your enlistment oath, in fact, you swear (or affirm) that you will obey the orders of the President of the United States and of other duly appointed officers. Officers are generally appointed by the President after being recommended by their branch of service, and that is why they are called commissioned officers. But there are other kinds of officers, including warrant officers and non-commissioned officers (Army sergeants and Navy petty officers are examples of non-commissioned officers).

Thus, members of the military services who refuse to do an assigned job or to obey a lawful order of the officer in charge of their

Military Times Magazine

INSIGNIA OF THE UNITED STATES ARMED FORCES

ENLISTED

E-1	E-2	E-3	E-4	E-5	E-6	E-7	E-8	E-9

NAVY

| SEAMAN RECRUIT | SEAMAN APPRENTICE | SEAMAN | PETTY OFFICER THIRD CLASS * | PETTY OFFICER SECOND CLASS* | PETTY OFFICER FIRST CLASS * | CHIEF PETTY OFFICER* | SENIOR CHIEF PETTY OFFICER* | MASTER CHIEF PETTY OFFICER * | MASTER CHIEF PETTY OFFICER OF THE NAVY* |

MARINES

| (no insignia) PRIVATE | PRIVATE FIRST CLASS | LANCE CORPORAL | CORPORAL | SERGEANT | STAFF SERGEANT | GUNNERY SERGEANT | FIRST SERGEANT | SERGEANT MAJOR | SERGEANT MAJOR OF THE MARINE CORPS |

| | | | | | | | MASTER SERGEANT | MASTER GUNNERY SERGEANT | |

ARMY

| (no insignia) PRIVATE | PRIVATE | PRIVATE FIRST CLASS | CORPORAL | SERGEANT | STAFF SERGEANT | SERGEANT FIRST CLASS | FIRST SERGEANT | COMMAND SERGEANT MAJOR | SERGEANT MAJOR OF THE ARMY |

| | | | SPECIALIST 4 | SPECIALIST 5 | SPECIALIST 6 | | MASTER SERGEANT | SERGEANT MAJOR | |

AIR FORCE

| (no insignia) AIRMAN BASIC | AIRMAN | AIRMAN FIRST CLASS | SERGEANT / SENIOR AIRMAN | STAFF SERGEANT | TECHNICAL SERGEANT | MASTER SERGEANT | SENIOR MASTER SERGEANT | CHIEF MASTER SERGEANT | CHIEF MASTER SERGEANT OF THE AIR FORCE |

* Gold Stripes indicate 12 or more years of good conduct.

Chart by Phyllis Cox and John Pack

M THE TIMES zine

INSIGNIA OF THE UNITED STATES ARMED FORCES
OFFICERS

O-1	O-2	O-3	O-4	O-5	O-6	O-7	O-8	O-9	O-10	SPECIAL

NAVY

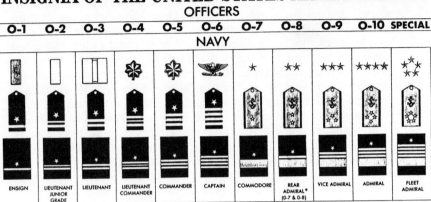

ENSIGN	LIEUTENANT JUNIOR GRADE	LIEUTENANT	LIEUTENANT COMMANDER	COMMANDER	CAPTAIN	COMMODORE	REAR ADMIRAL* (0-7 & 0-8)	VICE ADMIRAL	ADMIRAL	FLEET ADMIRAL

MARINES

SECOND LIEUTENANT	FIRST LIEUTENANT	CAPTAIN	MAJOR	LIEUTENANT COLONEL	COLONEL	BRIGADIER GENERAL	MAJOR GENERAL	LIEUTENANT GENERAL	GENERAL	

ARMY

SECOND LIEUTENANT	FIRST LIEUTENANT	CAPTAIN	MAJOR	LIEUTENANT COLONEL	COLONEL	BRIGADIER GENERAL	MAJOR GENERAL	LIEUTENANT GENERAL	GENERAL	GENERAL OF THE ARMY

AIR FORCE

SECOND LIEUTENANT	FIRST LIEUTENANT	CAPTAIN	MAJOR	LIEUTENANT COLONEL	COLONEL	BRIGADIER GENERAL	MAJOR GENERAL	LIEUTENANT GENERAL	GENERAL	GENERAL OF THE AIR FORCE

WARRANT

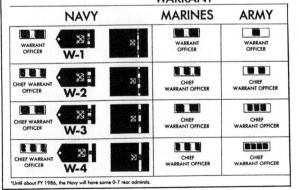

NAVY	MARINES	ARMY
WARRANT OFFICER W-1	WARRANT OFFICER	WARRANT OFFICER
CHIEF WARRANT OFFICER W-2	CHIEF WARRANT OFFICER	CHIEF WARRANT OFFICER
CHIEF WARRANT OFFICER W-3	CHIEF WARRANT OFFICER	CHIEF WARRANT OFFICER
CHIEF WARRANT OFFICER W-4	CHIEF WARRANT OFFICER	CHIEF WARRANT OFFICER

*Until about FY 1986, the Navy will have some 0-7 rear admirals.

COAST GUARD

Coast Guard enlisted rating badges are the same as the Navy's for grades E-1 through E-6. E-7s through E-9s have silver specialty marks, eagles and stars, and gold chevrons. The badge of the Master Chief Petty Officer of the Coast Guard has a gold chevron and specialty mark, a silver eagle and gold stars. Coast Guard officers use the same rank insignia as Navy officers. For all ranks, the gold Coast Guard shield on the uniform sleeve replaces the Navy star.

work unit are not penalized merely by having part of their pay withheld or by being fired, as might be the case in the civilian work force. Instead, they may be subject to disciplinary action or, even worse, to trial by a military court. Depending upon the circumstances, the charge might be malingering, insubordination, disrespect to a superior officer, or refusing to obey a lawful order. Repeated failure to conform to military standards of behavior may result in discharge from the service. Relatively few members of the military services ever find themselves in such situations. Preenlistment screening, the training and experience gained during basic training, and increased use of counseling all help to prevent such incidents.

In summary, each of the military services is more than a work force. Each is, rather, a special-purpose community that has its own goals and objectives and operates under its own laws and regulations. Members of a particular service are expected to identify with those objectives or missions, as defined by each service.

On the other hand, each service claims with some pride that it "takes care of our own." More about how this works out in practice is described in Chapter X, "Your Life in Military Service and Beyond."

CAREER PLANNING: EXAMINING A SLICE OF THE MILITARY JOB PIE

What we found in our pie chart was a group of broad occupational clusters. Actually, the armed forces offer more than 2,000 enlisted specialties. To make it easier to see what is involved, however, we shall examine only the 134 military occupations into which the twelve occupational clusters have been subdivided by the military services themselves.

In the following list military occupations are shown at the left and comparable civilian jobs at the right. Some military occupations, such as infantryman, do not have a civilian equivalent. In general, however, the discipline, close teamwork, and leadership training provided by those occupations may be useful in many civilian jobs. Moreover, many people in such military occupations obtain advanced education that may add to their qualifications for civilian employment.

We can pick any one, or several, of the 134 military occupations to illustrate the career planning process. Perhaps one of these selected at random may interest you. Remember, however, that these are starting positions. As you increase your skill level and demonstrate your ability on the job, opportunities will arise for advanced training, specialization, and promotion to a level where you may be super-

MILITARY OCCUPATIONS AND EQUIVALENT CIVILIAN JOBS

Military Occupations	*Civilian Job Titles*
ADMINISTRATIVE OCCUPATIONS	
Accounting Specialist	Accounting clerk, bookkeeper, audit clerk, statistical clerk
Administrative Support Specialist	Clerk-typist, administrative clerk, general clerk
Computer Operator	Computer operator
Court Reporter	Stenotype operator, court clerk
Data Entry Specialist	Keypunch operator, verifier
Dispatcher	Dispatcher (taxi, bus, etc.)
Flight Operations Specialist	Flight operations specialist, airline dispatch clerk
Lodging Specialist	Hotel clerk
Maintenance Data Analyst	Maintenance data analyst, aircraft-log clerk
Payroll Specialist	Payroll clerk
Personnel Specialist	Personnel clerk, employment clerk
Postal Specialist	Post-office clerk
Recruiting Specialist	Employment interviewer, personnel recruiter
Sales and Stock Specialist	Sales clerk, stock clerk
Secretary and Stenographer	Secretary, stenographer
Shipping and Receiving Specialist	Shipping and receiving clerk, cargo clerk, packager, industrial truck operator
Stock and Inventory Specialist	Stock-control clerk, parts clerk, inventory clerk, storekeeper, industrial truck operator
Telephone Operator	Telephone operator
Teletype Operator	Teletype operator
Trainer	Teacher, instructor, training representative, educational specialist
Transportation Specialist	Travel clerk, reservation clerk, gate agent, ground host/hostess, airplane flight attendant, transportation agent
COMBAT SPECIALTIES	
Artillery Crew Member	No direct equivalent
Combat Engineer	Construction worker, logger, demolition expert
Infantryman	No direct equivalent
Special Operations Force	Scuba diver, demolition expert, bomb disposal
Tank Crew Member	No direct equivalent
CONSTRUCTION OCCUPATIONS	
Blasting Specialist	"Blaster," or demolitions expert
Bricklayer, Concrete Mason	Bricklayer, cement mason
Building Electrician	Electrician
Carpenter	Carpenter
Iron Worker	Structural steel worker

CONSTRUCTION OCCUPATIONS (CONTINUED)

Paving Equipment Operator	Asphalt paving machine operator, concrete paving machine operator
Plumber and Pipe Fitter	Pipe fitter, plumber, aircraft mechanic, plumbing and hydraulics
Well Driller	Well-drill operator

ELECTRONIC AND ELECTRICAL INSTRUMENT REPAIR

Aircraft Electrician	Electrician, airplane
Data Processing Equipment Repairer	Electronics mechanic, avionics technician
Electrical Products Repairer	Electric motor repairer, electric motor winder, electromedical equipment repairer
Electronic Instrument Repairer	TV/radio repairer, avionics technician, electronics mechanic
Electronic Weapons Systems Repairer	Avionics technician, electronics mechanic, missile inspector
Line Installer/Repairer	Line installer/repairer, line erector, rigger, line maintainer, cable splicer, cable tester
Ordnance Mechanic	Gunsmith, aircraft armament mechanic, ordnance artificer
Photographic Equipment Repairer	Camera repairer, photographic equipment technician
Powerplant Electrician	Powerplant electrician
Precision Instrument Repairer	Watch repairer, instrument mechanic, instrument technician, calibrator, optical instrument inspector
Radar/Sonar Equipment Repairer	Radio mechanic, avionics technician, electronics mechanic
Radio Equipment Repairer	Radio mechanic, avionics technician, electronics mechanic, automatic equipment repairman
Ship Electrician	Electrician
Telephone Technician	Central office installer, central office repairer, PBX installer, telephone mechanic
Teletype Repairer	Automatic equipment technician, radio mechanic, avionics technician, electronics mechanic

ENGINEERING, SCIENCE, AND TECHNICAL

Air Traffic Controller	Air traffic controller
Broadcast/Recording Technician	Recording engineer, audio operator, sound mixer, video operator
Computer Programmer	Business programmer
Computer Systems Analyst	Systems analyst, electronic data processing
Drafter	Drafter, civil; drafter, structural

Emergency Management Specialist	Disaster control specialist
Environmental Health Specialist	Food and drug inspector, agricultural commodities inspector
Fuel/Chemical Laboratory Tehnician	Chemical laboratory technician, spectroscopist
Intelligence Specialist	Aerial-photograph interpreter, security agent
Legal Technician	Paralegal assistant
Mapping Technician	Cartographic drafter, topographic drafter, mosaicist, photogrammetrist
Nondestructive Tester	Nondestructive tester, radiographer
Radio Intelligence Operator	Radio intelligence operator
Radio Operator	Airline radio operator, radio officer, radio telegraph operator
Surveying Technician	Geodetic surveyor, chief of party, surveyor assistant
Weather Observer	Weather observer, weather clerk, assistant oceanographer

HEALTH CARE

Cardiopulmonary/EEG Technician	EKG technician, cardiopulmonary technologist, EEG technician
Dental Specialist	Dental assistant, dental hygienist
Medical Laboratory Technician	Medical technologist, cytotechnologist, hematologist, tissue technologist
Medical Record Technician	Hospital admitting clerk, medical record clerk
Medical Service Technician	Medical assistant, physician assistant, emergency medical technician
Nursing Technician	Orderly, pyschiatric technician, licensed practical nurse
Occupational Therapy Specialist	Occupational therapy aide
Operating Room Technician	Surgical technician
Optometric Technician	Optometric assistant
Orthopedic Technician	Orthopedic assistant,
Orthiotic Technician	Othiotics assistant, othiotist
Pharmacy Technician	Pharmacy technician, pharmacy assistant
Physical Therapy Specialist	Physical therapy aide, physical-integration practitioner
Radiologic (X-ray) Technician	Radiologic technologist, radiation therapist, nuclear medical technician
Respiratory Specialist	Respiratory therapist

HUMAN SERVICES

Caseworker, Counselor	Human relations counselor, drug/alcohol counselor, caseworker, counselor

HUMAN SERVICES (CONTINUED)

Recreation Specialist	Recreation leader
Religious Program Specialist	Director, religious programs

MACHINE OPERATOR AND PRECISION WORK

Boiler Technician	Boilerhouse mechanic
Clothing and Fabric Repairer	Garment fitter, alteration tailor, canvas repairer
Compressed Gas Technician	Compressed plant operator, oxygen plant operator, compressed gas test technician
Dental Laboratory Technician	Dental laboratory technician
Machinist	Machinist, machine setup operator
Optician	Dispensing optician, optician
Photoprocessing Specialist	Film developer, print developer, quality control technician
Power Plant Operator	Boiler operator, diesel plant operator, stationary engineer, power-reactor operator
Printing Specialist	Plate maker, stripper, lithographic photographer, offset press operator
Sheet Metal Worker	Sheet metal worker
Shipfitter	Shipfitter, marine services technician
Survival Equipment Specialist	Parachute rigger, survival equipment repairer
Water and Sewage Treatment Plant Operator	Pump station operator, water treatment plant operator, waste-water treatment plant operator
Welder	Arc welder, welder-fitter, weld inspector

MEDIA AND PUBLIC AFFAIRS

Audiovisual Production Specialist	Audiovisual production specialist
Graphic Designer and Illustrator	Graphic arts technician, graphic designer, illustrator
Interpreter and Translator	Interpreter, translator
Motion Picture Camera Operator	Motion picture camera operator, aerial photographer
Musician	Musician (instrumental), singer, arranger, composer, conductor
Photographer	Aerial photographer, still photographer, photojournalist
Radio and TV Announcer	Announcer, disk jockey
Reporter and Newswriter	Reporter, newswriter, newscaster, copywriter, screen writer, editorial assistant, editor

SERVICE OCCUPATIONS

Barber	Barber
Corrections Specialist	Corrections officer
Detective	Detective, private investigator, security officer

Firefighter	Firefighter, inspector
Food Service Specialist	Chef, cook, baker, butcher
Military Police	Security guard, police officer, deputy sheriff

TRANSPORTATION AND MATERIAL HANDLING

Air Crew Member	No direct equivalent; some skills may be useful in civil aviation occupations
Aircraft Launch and Recovery Specialist	No direct equivalent; some skills may be useful in ground operations at civil airfields
Boat Operator	Motorboat operator, tugboat captain
Cargo Specialist	Stevedore, winch-driver, industrial truck driver
Construction Equipment Operator	Operating engineer
Flight Engineer	Flight engineer
Petroleum Supply Specialist	Tank-car inspector, cargo inspector, pumper-gauger, pipeline worker, station engineer, crane operator

VEHICLE AND MACHINERY MECHANIC

Aircraft Mechanic	Aircraft body repairer, airframe/power plant mechanic, aircraft heating/ventilating mechanic
Automobile Mechanic	Automobile mechanic, transmission mechanic, radiator mechanic, carburetor mechanic
Automotive Body Repairer	Automobile body repairer, painter
Diver	Diver
Engine Mechanic	Diesel mechanic, gas-engine mechanic, motorboat mechanic, tractor mechanic, marine engine mechanic
Heating and Cooling Mechanic	Refrigeration mechanic, environmental control system installer/repairer
Heavy Equipment Mechanic	Construction equipment mechanic, tracked-vehicle mechanic
Marine Engine Mechanic	Maintenance mechanic, engine
Office Machine Repairer	Office machine servicer
Powerhouse Mechanic	Powerhouse mechanic
Rigger	Rigger

vising other military personnel in the same occupational field. Now, consider this list:

Accounting Specialist
Teletype Operator
Combat Engineer
Plumber and Pipefitter
Electronic Instrument Repairer

Computer Programmer
Dental Specialist
Religious Program Specialist
Machinist
Interpreter and Translator
Food Service Specialist
Construction Equipment Operator
Office Machine Repairer

In this list, representing the twelve broad occupational clusters, there seems to be something for almost everyone. Each occupation has one or more equivalents in the civilian work force. Moreover, with the exception of Combat Engineer, each occupation is open to women.

Perhaps your eyes light up at the first entry: Accounting Specialist. You've been taking business courses in high school, and you especially liked accounting. You would really like to go to college and major in business administration, but you know that your parents cannot afford the tuition right now. The jobs in the accounting field in your town are not particularly interesting. Maybe you should see what the military services have to offer. Certainly, you need more information. What do you do next?

All of the military occupations are also listed in Appendix C, along with:

1. The services that offer the occupational specialty.
2. The number of military people in the occupation.
3. The estimated number of new entrants needed each year.
4. A guide to the ASVAB scores needed to qualify for entry.
5. Training requirements for assignment in the occupation.
6. An estimate of growth in the number of jobs in the occupation, for the civilian work force, through 1995.

In Appendix C, under Accounting Specialist, you find that all five military services need accounting specialists. In fact, they have about 10,100 of them, and about 1,010 positions are available to new recruits every year.

Read further, and you discover that you should have a score of between 53 and 61 in the business and clerical area of the ASVAB to qualify for this occupational field. Between eight and twelve weeks of entry-level training is required. Moreover, prospects for civilian employment in the accounting field are good should you decide not to make a career of military service.

Perhaps you are more interested in becoming a skilled machinist. Follow the approach already used to locate Machinist in Appendix C. You find that all military services need machinists, but you also notice something different about the Army and the Navy. In the column for each of these services is the symbol (A). This means that they may have apprenticeship programs in one or more of the specialties included under the military occupation of Machinist. The U.S. Department of Labor has agreed to accept technical and on-the-job training in the appropriate military service as a full-fledged apprenticeship program leading to certification as journeyman. The program is demanding, but the journeyman certificate is worth working for. It is accepted by both trade unions and civilian employers as evidence of an advanced skill level in a particular field of work.

Looking further in Appendix C, you find that 5,500 jobs for machinists are to be found in the military services, and the services require about 560 replacements (recruits) each year. The required score in the ASVAB mechanical and crafts field is quite high: between 52 and 62. Entry-level training provided by the military services lasts ten to twelve weeks. Finally, the Department of Labor estimates growth of about 26 percent in the number of civilian jobs in the machinist category through 1995, a growth figure that is about average. You decide to look into this situation, because you know that you would otherwise have to spend an expensive year or more in a vocational institution to get the same training. Even then, you might not be able to find a job.

As the next step, you should consult your high school career counselor. He or she can probably tell you where and when you can take the ASVAB. Providing you score well on the essential occupation area of the test, you will have a pretty good idea of your chances for assignment to a specialty within the military occupation you have chosen to explore. Next you should visit one or more of the armed services recruiters near you to hear what they have to say.

Before you begin, however, you should have some idea of which service you might prefer. You should also find out what training and educational opportunities may be available to you in that service. Once you enlist in a military service, you have started a process that could occupy you for twenty or more years of your adult life. Along the way, assuming that you have the necessary energy and willpower, you may even be able to achieve journeyman status in your career field or earn a college degree.

Chapter **IV**

Educational Opportunities in the Military Services

The military services collectively offer exceptional educational opportunities, ranging from introductory military instruction to cooperative programs with recognized universities at the highest postgraduate level.

At any given time about ten percent of the members of the services are engaged in formal military-specific training at hundreds of schools run by the services themselves. Tens of thousands of others are enrolled in off-duty advanced educational programs of a civilian nature. Some of these programs are operated by the services themselves, such as the Community College of the Air Force and the Marine Corps Institute. Others are run by cooperating colleges and universities that offer degree programs in facilities located on military installations.

Thousands of enlisted men and women are able to complete at least some college studies each year under full-time resident programs that provide scholarships or other forms of financial assistance. Those who complete four-year degree programs may be eligible for further training to become officers. Officers in all the military services may be afforded opportunities for full-time graduate studies leading to advanced degrees at civilian universities.

Each year, the military services also award scholarships to thousands of civilian students who are engaged in undergraduate and postgraduate studies. Most of these scholarships are associated with officer commissioning programs.

As a result of this emphasis on vocational and general education, the educational level of the 2.1 million members of the military services exceeds that of the general population of the United States. About ninety-six percent of all enlisted personnel have at least a high school–level education; nearly twenty percent of these have some college-level education. It is estimated that more than 90 percent of career enlisted personnel have completed some college-level education by the time they leave the service; many have earned bachelor's degrees; more have earned associate degrees.

The educational level for officers is even more impressive, even though a college degree is generally a prerequisite for a commission (but not for appointment as a warrant officer). Among all the commissioned and warrant officers for whom statistics are available, nearly 94 percent are college graduates; almost 40 percent of these hold advanced degrees, many of which were earned during active military service.

In this chapter we shall summarize the many "civilian" educational opportunities offered by the military services.

FEDERAL SERVICE ACADEMIES

The service academies operated by the military services are probably the first to come to mind when military educational opportunities are mentioned. The four academies are the United States Air Force Academy, Colorado Springs, Colorado; the United States Coast Guard Academy, New London, Connecticut; the United States Military Academy, West Point, New York; and the United States Naval Academy, Annapolis, Maryland, which also trains officers for the United States Marine Corps.

Actually, each of these academies is best thought of as a commissioning program operated by the respective military service for the development of junior officers. As a group, the four academies contribute only about fifteen percent of all new officers who enter on active military service each year. Academy graduates are, of course, somewhat special: They form the professional core of the military service. For our purposes, however, we shall consider the academies largely as important institutions in the complex "civilian" educational system operated by, or supported by, the military services.

All the service academies offer four-year college programs leading to a bachelor of science degree, as well as a full range of extracurricular activities, including intercollegiate sports. Tuition, medical care, and board and room are free to students. The educational facilities, programs, and faculty (usually a mix of military officers and civilians) meet or exceed the standards of the appropriate regional college accreditation agencies. The Air Force Academy, for example, compares itself to Stanford University, Harvard University, the University of California at Berkeley, and the Massachusetts Institute of Technology.

Generally the academies offer a choice of undergraduate academic majors similar to those of civilian colleges and universities. Each

Cadets in class at the United States Air Force Academy.

student must, however, complete a core curriculum prescribed by the academy. The core curricula tend to emphasize mathematics and science.

No graduate programs are offered by the academies; but academic standards are high, and many graduates compete successfully each year for Rhodes scholarships, Guggenheim fellowships, Marshall fellowships, National Science Foundation scholarships, and others that permit them to pursue graduate studies in the United States and abroad. Up to two percent of each graduating class of the Army, Navy, and Air Force academies are sent for training in the medical and health professions under fully funded joint service programs. Academy graduates who do not qualify for scholarships or other immediate graduate training are usually eligible for graduate study at civilian universities after initial periods of active service.

Military Training at the Academies

The students at the academies wear military uniforms and are under military discipline. They are known as cadets or midshipmen, but they have no military status outside the academy. The allowance each receives, about five hundred dollars a month, is not considered military pay. In addition to the normal program of academic studies, the cadets receive basic military training prior to their first academic semester and throughout the four years, interspersed with the normal academic coursework. After the first year, the emphasis is on the development of leadership and management qualities.

Upperclassmen devote most of their summers to advanced military instruction approximately equal to that provided by the officer training schools of the various services. Students of the service academies, however, receive expanded opportunities during the summer training sessions. Advanced West Point cadets, for example, may elect training in airborne, air assault, arctic warfare, and jungle warfare specialties; others may be assigned, as noncommissioned officers, to conduct recruit training at regular Army installations throughout the U.S. Air Force Academy upperclassmen participate in service-wide command post exercises, receive preflight indoctrination, or take airborne training, among other options. Annapolis midshipmen are exposed to operations at sea, aboard ship. Coast Guard cadets may participate in actual Coast Guard operations at shore stations and aboard ships; they receive flight indoctrination; and, as a special experience, they cruise at sea aboard the Coast Guard's square-rigger the *Eagle*.

Graduates of the service academies are commissioned in the regular component of the appropriate service and are required to serve on active duty for five years. Approximately sixty to seventy percent of all academy graduates remain in service and pursue military careers.

Qualifications and Admission Procedures

Admission to the service academies is open to civilian men and women and to active-duty and reserve enlisted members of the military services who are at least seventeen years of age and will not have had their twenty-second birthday by July 1 of the year of admission. Applicants must also be citizens of the United States, unmarried, of good moral character, and able to meet the academic, physical, and medical requirements. Applicants who have legal dependents of any kind are disqualified.

Appointment to any of the four academies is highly competitive. Overall academic preparation and physical condition are vitally important to success after admission. Academic qualifications are based on scores obtained on the Scholastic Aptitude Test (SAT) and the American College Testing Program (ACT), plus a review of school records. Participation in school athletic programs, student government, clubs, and other extracurricular activities is highly desirable. Medical examinations are provided by the service after academic qualifications have been evaluated.

Except for the Coast Guard Academy, applicants for admission to the service academies must be nominated for appointment. Appointments to the Coast Guard Academy are made on the basis of nationwide competition. Eligible civilians and members of the military services compete on an equal basis. Completed applications and all test scores must be received by the Coast Guard Academy no later than December 15 of the year before the next class begins; thus, students should contact the Director of Admissions of the Coast Guard Academy (see Appendix E) during the spring semester of their junior year in high school.

Nominations for the other academies must be obtained from the sources listed below. Prospective applicants may write directly to an academy (or to all) to request a precandidate questionnaire and details of procedures (see Appendix E for addresses). This request should be sent during the spring semester of the junior year in high school. If you have already graduated from high school, make the request in March or April of the year before you wish to attend the academy.

Nominations may be obtained from any of the following, depending upon the category of the prospective applicant:

1. Vice President of the United States: Any applicant who meets the basic eligibility requirements (ten nominations for each academy vacancy).
2. Members of Congress: Any applicant who meets the basic eligibility requirements. Apply to the Representative or either of the Senators from your legal home of record; or you may apply to all three. This is the largest source of nominations; each member of Congress can make ten nominations for each vacancy.
3. Delegates to Congress: Bona fide residents of the District of Columbia, the Virgin Islands, American Samoa, and Guam should write to those representatives in Washington, D.C.
4. Governor of Puerto Rico: Qualified applicants who are native-born Puerto Ricans.
5. Resident Commissioner of Puerto Rico: Qualified applicants who are residents of Puerto Rico.
6. Commissioner, Panama Canal Commission: Qualified applicants who are residents of the Panama Canal Zone.
7. Director of Admissions at academy of choice: Qualified applicants who have military affiliations, specifically:

a. Presidential nominees: Children of career members of the military services, active or reserve, who are:
  (1) serving on active duty and have at least eight years' continuous service; or
  (2) retired from active duty with pay; or
  (3) deceased retired veterans.
b. Children of deceased or one hundred percent disabled veterans whose death or disability was determined to be service-connected.
c. Children of military personnel or civilian employees of the federal government who are officially listed as missing or captured.
d. Children of Medal of Honor recipients (such persons are guaranteed admission if otherwise qualified).
e. (Through ROTC detachment commander or senior military instructor) Junior ROTC or college ROTC students, and students at designated Honor Military or Naval Schools.
f. (Through military channels) Active and reserve enlisted men and women. Note that applications from this category may be sent only to the academy identified with the military service in which serving. Consult service regulations for appropriate form.

Details of the procedures for application and for nomination, if required, are contained in the catalog of each service academy. Normally, a catalog, application forms, and other information are sent to you when you request the precandidate questionnaire from the Director of Admissions of an academy.

Serious candidates are advised to explore every possible route to an appointment. In many cases, application is made to several academies. The possibility that you may fall into two or more categories should not be overlooked. Some candidates who have not been selected from a general category have enlisted in a military service (active or reserve), reapplied, and then been accepted from the new category.

Prospective candidates who have not obtained an appointment the first time, or who are not fully qualified for academic reasons, can enhance their chances by attending one of the preparatory schools operated by the military services or by civilian agencies.

Through the Back Door: Academy Preparatory Schools

Each of the service academies except the Coast Guard Academy operates a preparatory school that enables prospective candidates to improve their English, science, and mathematics. The preparatory schools of the Army, Navy, and Air Force offer nine-month courses (August to May). Physical conditioning and military training are included in the programs. Students must meet the prerequisites for appointment to the academy. Completion of a preparatory school course does not, however, guarantee appointment.

The preparatory schools operated by the Air Force and the Navy emphasize preparation of enlisted men and women of the respective service, though civilians may also apply for the Naval Academy school. In the case of the Air Force, civilians are not allowed to apply; those who failed to secure appointment because of academic deficiencies but otherwise show outstanding potential are automatically selected to attend the preparatory school. Applications for the Army's preparatory school are accepted from both civilians and enlisted members of all Army components, active or reserve.

The Air Force Preparatory School is on the grounds of the Air Force Academy, in Colorado Springs. The Army school is at Fort Monmouth, New Jersey; the Navy preparatory school is in Newport, Rhode Island. Inquiries may be sent to the addresses given in Appendix E.

The Navy has another academic preparatory program that offers Navy and Marine enlisted personnel up to twelve months of intensive studies that make them competitive for selection to the Naval Academy or to the Naval ROTC Scholarship Program. The program, called BOOST for Broadened Opportunity for Officer Selection and Training, is given in San Diego, California. It is also available as an enlistment option to new enlistees in the Navy or Marine Corps.

Prospective civilian candidates for admission to the Air Force Academy who need additional academic preparation may obtain it from two private, nonprofit agencies. One, the Falcon Foundation, awards scholarships to selected civilian preparatory schools. The other, the General Henry H. Arnold Educational Fund, provides educational assistance to the children of Air Force personnel. See Appendix E for addresses.

RESERVE OFFICERS TRAINING CORPS

About forty percent of the newly commissioned officers who enter the military services each year are graduates of colleges and universities that offer military training under the Reserve Officers Training Corps (ROTC) program. ROTC programs for the Army, Navy, Marine Corps, and Air Force are available at many colleges and universities; see Appendix D.

The ROTC programs are the largest single source of officers for the Army, Navy, and Air Force. Both men and women are eligible for ROTC training. Special ROTC programs are available for nurses; the Air Force ROTC Program also enables some graduates to attend medical school under the Armed Forces Health Professions Scholarship Program after they have received their commission. Each service also has special provisions for participation in the ROTC program by active-duty and reserve enlisted personnel.

Graduates of ROTC programs generally receive commissions in the reserve component of each service; they may be obligated to serve on active duty following commissioning.

Commissioning terms vary among the services. Some distinguished graduates and most scholarship recipients receive regular commission. Graduates who receive reserve commissions are sometimes able to convert to regular status while they are serving on active duty.

Program of the Reserve Officers Training Corps

Participation in ROTC during your college years enables you to acquire sufficient military training and background to qualify for a commission as an officer upon graduation without any significant interruption of your other studies. Your choice of a college major is not restricted in any way. You sign up for ROTC during registration just as you would for any other course. No military obligation is involved during the first two years unless you are a scholarship student.

The ROTC program is divided into two sections. The two-year first section involves basic military training and is open to anyone who can meet ROTC physical standards and will not have reached his or her thirty-fifth birthday by the time requirements for a commission are expected to be met. Military training during these two years includes both formal classes and field training.

Admission to the second phase of ROTC may be competitive. If accepted, you begin more professional military studies. Depending upon the service, summer training sessions of varied length are also required, usually between the junior and senior years. It is possible to enroll only for the second phase, but this may require attendance at a four- to six-week basic military training program, unless you have had prior military experience.

During the first two years, you receive no remuneration for participation in the ROTC program. In the advanced phase, however, you receive a monthly stipend of one hundred dollars and are paid for attendance at summer camp. If you complete the program you receive a commission in the reserve component of the service. After graduation and commissioning, you are assigned to a reserve unit unless you volunteer for active duty.

ROTC Scholarship Programs

If you are serious about a military career, you may be able to obtain an ROTC scholarship that covers the costs of tuition, laboratory and incidental fees, and textbooks. In addition, you qualify for a small monthly allowance and are paid at the pay grade of E-5 during required summer training. Uniforms are also provided.

You can earn a regular commission in the Navy or Marine Corps in this way. ROTC training under a scholarship program may also lead to a Regular Army commission, depending upon the final evaluation of your performance and capabilities. In any case, you are obligated to serve on active duty for a minimum of four years; longer if, for example, you elect flight training.

Thousands of four-year ROTC scholarships are available each year to high school seniors. The application period is generally between April and November of the year before the student expects to enter college. Applicants may apply to the Army, the Navy, or the Air Force. Scholarships of shorter duration are usually available only to students who have already completed some college. For details of these programs, write to the service or services that interest you (see Appendix E).

CONTINUING EDUCATION FOR ENLISTED PERSONNEL

The opportunities for enlisted men and women to continue non-military education while in active service are almost unlimited. The military services offer tuition assistance (up to 75 percent) to part-time off-duty students in local colleges and universities. Some of the services have their own educational institutions: the Community College of the Air Force, for example, and the Navy Campus, which allows Navy people to pursue all levels of education and training, wherever they are stationed.

Military personnel on active duty may also earn college credit for technical training provided by the armed services or by examination in about fifty vocational and academic fields. Other programs, such as the Air Force Bootstrap program, allow selected noncommissioned officers to spend up to a year at a civilian college, with full pay and allowances, to complete requirements for a degree.

A service-wide program, Servicemembers Opportunity Colleges (SOC), includes more than 400 two- and four-year colleges and universities that offer programs specially geared to service members at about 500 military installations in the United States and elsewhere. Participants in the SOC program have adopted simplified admissions requirements (including accepting GED credentials) and streamlined administrative procedures; special provisions facilitate the transfer of credits from one institution to another; and college credit may be awarded for some aspects of military training.

Thus, it is possible to earn a college degree even though you are reassigned every year or two to another part of the country or the world. For example, Southern Illinois University offers under-graduate degree programs at sixty-two military installations in twenty-four states and two foreign countries. The programs available in 1986 were Aviation Management, Electronics Management, Industrial Technology, Health Care Management, and Occupational Education.

The opportunities for advanced nonmilitary education in pursuit of an academic degree increase with length of service. The rewards, both in personal and in professional terms, are many. Those planning to enter a military service should consult their recruiters about specific programs.

THE NEW GI BILL

A relatively recent development in the educational field is the so-called New GI Bill, a program administered by the Veterans Administration that allows enlisted men and women to accumulate funds for college study while serving on active duty.

Discussion of this program may seem more appropriate in Chapter X on veterans' benefits. Because new recruits must indicate their intention to participate in the program within a specified time after entering military service, it seems necessary to mention it here.

Participants in the program contribute up to one hundred dollars from their pay each month to establish a college fund. The monthly contribution is matched by the government, at the ratio of two to one or even better. This money may only be used after the participant has been discharged from military service.

Opinions vary about the significance of this program, but participation may be of great interest to a recently discharged veteran who accumulated some college credit during his or her active military service and wishes to complete requirements for a degree.

EDUCATIONAL OPPORTUNITIES AT THE OFFICER LEVEL

The thrust of advanced education for most officers is in the direction of graduate degrees. All the military services offer career officers opportunities for full-time graduate study in civilian universities, generally at the level of the master's degree but often up to the doctorate. Officers may, of course, participate in the off-duty educational programs already mentioned, including tuition assistance programs.

Professional Training

Institutions at the graduate level are operated by the Navy and the Air Force. The Navy Post-Graduate School in Monterey, California, offers many courses on campus and coordinates the attendance of Navy officers at off-campus sites. The Air Force Institute of Technology, Dayton, Ohio, offers resident programs in engineering and logistics and Air Force–sponsored degree programs at civilian universities.

The Uniformed Services University of Health Sciences, which trains physicians and other medical officers for the Army, Navy, and Air Force, is another graduate-level institution entirely under military control. While it is necessary to be a member of the military to attend the university, the fact is that civilian applicants are appointed second lieutenant or ensign and are paid a salary while they study for a medical degree.

Another graduate-level medical program available under the auspices of the Army, the Navy, and the Air Force is the Armed Forces Health Professions Scholarship Program. Participants in this program must be enrolled in or accepted for admission to an accredited school of medicine or osteopathy. They are commissioned second lieutenant or ensign in the inactive reserve. Tuition, fees, and related expenses are paid by the military service, along with a stipend of more than five hundred dollars a month during the school year. Participants are required to attend active-duty training each year and must serve a minimum of three years on active duty following graduation from medical school.

Both the Army and the Air Force offer active-duty officers the opportunity to attend law school to obtain a legal degree, while drawing full pay and allowances. Following the degree, the officers are assigned to Judge Advocate functions.

Academic Credit for Service Colleges

This chapter has generally avoided mention of service-oriented schools operated by the military, but it would be unfair to suggest that the courses given by them have no academic content. In particular, the staff colleges and war colleges of each of the military services contribute much to expanding intellectual horizons. Though most of these institutions do not provide degree programs, some academic credit may be earned. Attendance at some of the war colleges may qualify students for advanced degrees.

Part II

THE MILITARY SERVICES OF THE UNITED STATES

Introduction
The Department of Defense

The Department of Defense is the executive department of the United States government, which since 1949 has been responsible for providing the military forces required to protect and defend the United States, its institutions, and its interests at home and abroad. The Secretary of Defense, a civilian, is responsible to the President, who is also Commander in Chief of all armed forces. Under the authority of the President, the Secretary of Defense is responsible for policies, direction, and control of the Department of Defense and of the separately organized Departments of the Army, Navy, and Air Force.

The United States Coast Guard is also organized separately, but it operates as a service of the Department of Transportation during peacetime. In time of war, however, the Coast Guard may operate under the control of the United States Navy. For purposes of this section, therefore, we shall consider the Coast Guard a full-fledged military service. And, indeed, in recent years it has often been on the front line, so to speak, as a result of its aggressive pursuit in distant seas of narcotics smugglers, among other things.

The Department of Defense was created to coordinate the defense program of the United States. In furtherance of that aim it has established numerous military commands, organizations, agencies, and schools. A brief introduction to some of them should help you to understand how complex the country's defense organization really is.

What may be even more important to you, as a future member of one of the armed services, is that the joint-service nature of Department of Defense (DOD) commands and agencies helps to lower the barriers of custom and tradition that historically have surrounded each military service. Over the years, national defense objectives have increasingly replaced individual service objectives, for example. Joint-service procedures have increasingly led to improved efficiency. As a member of one military service, you may very likely find yourself living, studying, or working alongside members of other services, almost from the start. As you advance in training and experience, your colleagues may even be members of allied or foreign military forces.

Probably the most familiar of the organizations under DOD control are the so-called unified and specified commands. Unified commands are composed of forces from two or more military services and are organized geographically to carry out broad, continuing missions. Commanders of unified commands are usually Army generals or Navy admirals, but they report to the President, through the Joint Chiefs of Staff and the Secretary of Defense, rather than to their service chief.

The number of unified commands varies from time to time. In 1986 the six unified commands and their headquarters were as follows.

U.S. European Command (CINCEUR, Stuttgart, Germany)
U.S. Atlantic Command (CINCLANT, Norfolk, Virginia)
U.S. Pacific Command (CINCPAC, Honolulu, Hawaii)
U.S. Southern Command (CINCSOUTH, Quarry Heights, Panama)
U.S. Readiness Command (READCOM, MacDill AFB, Florida)
U.S. Central Command (CENTCOM, MacDill AFB, Florida)

You can probably guess that these unifed commands are teams of units drawn from the Army (land forces), the Air Force (to support the land forces and to control the air space above the battlefield), and the Navy and Marines (to keep open sea lanes needed for supply ships, for example, or to protect or support land forces).

The specified commands, on the other hand, are normally made up of forces from a single service and are organized according to function. The four specified commands in 1986 were all commanded by Air Force generals:

Aerospace Defense Command (Colorado Springs, Colorado)
Military Airlift Command (Scott AFB, Illinois)
Strategic Air Command (Omaha, Nebraska)
U.S. Space Command (Colorado Springs, Colorado)

Specified commands are not usually limited to any geographical area. Strategic Air Command aircraft may be flying right now anywhere in the world, for example. Moreover, specified commands frequently must operate twenty-four hours a day to carry out their mission.

The Department of Defense has also established a score or so agencies and field activities responsible for coordinating military activities in such areas as research, logistics, public information, communications, medical and health programs, intelligence and security, and dependent schools abroad.

Finally, in this brief survey of Department of Defense activities, are the joint-service schools around the country. Outstanding among them is the National Defense University, an institution for senior military officers and civilian government officials. It includes the National War College, the Industrial College of the Armed Forces, and the DOD Computer Institute, all in Washington, D.C., and the Armed Forces Staff College, in Norfolk, Virginia. The others are concerned largely with advanced management training for senior military members and civilian employees of the military services.

Chapter **V**

The United States Army

The United States Army is the oldest of the military services of the United States. Established on June 14, 1775, by the Continental Congress, the Army is actually older than the Republic. Of course, many things have changed over the years, and early military leaders like George Washington and Nathaniel Green would hardly recognize the modern high-tech American Army.

On the other hand, tradition plays a role in any military organization, and the Army is no exception. The Third Infantry Regiment, nicknamed "The Old Guard" and now serving the national capital in various ceremonial roles, occasionally stages colorful events that recall the past. Wearing uniforms of the Continental Army era, the Old Guard marches to "Yankee Doodle Dandy," played by the regiment's own fife and drum corps. If you look closely, however, you will see that the regimental flag is partly obscured by a fluttering mass of faded ribbons. These are the "battle streamers" that testify to a combat record spanning much of our two-hundred-year history as an independent nation. For tradition celebrates continuity, not just old age.

Add motivation and training to tradition and continuity and you will have captured the essential nature of the modern United States Army. The Army's slogan these days is "Army: Be All You Can Be," and those are more than mere words. The Army offers outstanding opportunities for career-minded individuals, along with the training that enables each to realize his or her maximum potential, whether in the senior enlisted ranks or as an officer. Let's take a brief look at how the Army is organized and where its units and people are located, for more than one third of the people serving in the active Army are located outside the United States.

ORGANIZATION AND DEPLOYMENT OF THE ARMY

The United States Army is not only the oldest of our military services; it is also the largest, with more than 780 thousand men and women in uniform. In addition, about one million men and women serve in the reserve components (the Army Reserve and the Army National Guard). The sheer size of the establishment is enough to suggest that the Army is a very complicated organization, and, indeed, it is.

As a military service, the Army is organized and trained to fight on land. But the basic mission of the Army, to defend the United States, its institutions, and its vast territories, can be an overwhelming one. The demands of modern warfare force the Army to take to the air, and even to the sea at times, to accomplish its mission on the ground. A standing joke among members of this land-based service is that the Army has more aircraft than the Air Force and more boats and ships than the Navy.

Moreover, the Army's mission has been expanded in recent decades to include the defense of American interests around the world. Today, about 275 thousand Army men and women are stationed overseas, in Europe, East Asia, the Pacific Basin, and Latin America. They are there largely to satisfy the terms of half a dozen defense treaties concluded between the United States and allies since the end of World War II. Several thousand others are serving around

U.S. ARMY PHOTO

A chow line at a United States Army installation.

the world as military assistance advisers to foreign governments, as members of American embassies (military attachés and their staffs), and in other capacities.

Hence, both the Army's mission and the advanced technology of contemporary warfare have combined to influence the organization and operations of the modern United States Army.

Army Headquarters

The Department of the Army has operated since 1949 as one of the three military departments of the Department of Defense. Army Headquarters is located in Washington, D.C., in the Pentagon. A civilian Secretary of the Army, appointed by the President, is responsible for the organization, administration, and operation of the Army and for other activities that may be assigned by the President or by the Secretary of Defense.

Among the additional activities for which the Secretary of the Army is responsible are the civil government of designated foreign areas (including maintenance and operation of the Panama Canal) and the civil-works program of the Army Corps of Engineers (supervising inland waterways, building and managing flood control projects, for example). The Department of the Army is also involved with civil defense, disaster relief, military assistance to federal, state, and local governments, and emergency medical air transportation.

Within the Department of the Army, the Chief of Staff, the senior Army General, is the senior military commander and the principal military adviser to the Secretary. He presides over the Army General Staff, a group of senior Generals who assist him with his responsibilities for planning, developing, carrying out, and evaluating Army programs. Each of the Deputy (or Assistant) Chiefs of Staff is assigned specific responsibilities in fields such as personnel matters, intelligence, military operations and plans, logistics (procurement, supply, and maintenance of weapons and military equipment), and research and development.

The Army Headquarters also has a Special Staff that includes the Adjutant General (administration), the Surgeon General, the Chief of Chaplains (morale and religious affairs), the Judge Advocate General (legal affairs), the Chief of Army Reserve, and others. Special Staff members and agencies may be called upon by the Secretary of the Army or the Chief of Staff for advice on technical matters related to their special fields of interest. The chiefs of the various technical services (see below) may also be involved in plans and programs developed by Army Headquarters.

Components of the Army

When most people speak about "the Army," they usually mean the active-duty forces. However, the adoption of the "One Army" concept in the 1970s expanded the definition to include the Army National Guard and the Army Reserve.

At any given time, moreover, the active-duty force includes Army Reserve and Army National Guard individuals. In time of war or other emergency, Army Reserve and National Guard units also may be included in the active Army establishment. Therefore, they must be organized, equipped, and trained just as the active Army is. During the recent U.S. intervention in Grenada, for example, civil-affairs units of the Army Reserve were placed on temporary active duty to support the joint-service task force that carried out the operation.

Within the total Army organization, officers and men alike are assigned to branches. As a general rule, each branch is organized to support the overall mission of the Army, and each branch has its own history and traditions. The branches of the Army may operate schools and other training activities, carry out research and development programs, provide equipment and supplies, and control the military careers of Army personnel assigned to them, especially in the case of Army officers. An important consideration for anyone who plans to enter the Army is to have some idea of the functions of the branch to which he or she may be assigned.

The twenty-two Army branches include the combat arms (Armor, Infantry, Field Artillery), the combat support branches (Engineers, Military Police, Air Defense Artillery), and the technical and administrative services, usually designated as corps. Typical technical services are the Medical Corps, the Signal Corps, the Ordnance Corps, the Transportation Corps, the Quartermaster Corps, and the Corps of Engineers. Among the administrative services are the Adjutant General Corps, the Finance Corps, the Judge Advocate General Corps, and the Chaplain Corps.

At times, the distinction between the combat arms and some of the technical services may seem hazy. The Engineer Corps, for instance, includes Combat Engineers—who are trained to fight as infantry. Medical Corps personnel provide services to front-line units. Personnel of the Tranportation Corps operate watercraft in support of amphibious operations.

Army personnel wear branch insignia, most of which are traditional and symbolic. Two crossed muskets identify infantrymen, for example. Two signal flags (of the kind used for sending messages

A Specialist 4th class transmits a teletype message.

between ground units before radio was invented—and still used by the Navy) are crossed on the Signal Corps insignia. Armor superimposes a tank on the traditional crossed swords used by the old horse cavalry; the Armor branch was once known as the Armored Cavalry.

The Major Army Commands

As the name suggests, the Headquarters of the Department of the Army provides overall direction for the Army. The operating forces are organized into commands that have functional or tactical roles. The major Army functional commands include the Health Services Command (administers Army hospitals), the Military Traffic Management Command, the Intelligence and Security Command, the Corps of Engineers, Army Materiel Command (procurement and supply of equipment), the Criminal Investigation Command, and the Information Systems Command. These seven commands provide support services to the entire Army, and they employ large numbers of civilians as well as military personnel.

Other Army commands have tactical missions limited to specific geographic regions. Included are the Military District of Washington (Washington, D.C.), U.S. Army Europe, U.S. Army Japan, Eighth U.S. Army (Korea), U.S. Army Western Command (Hawaii), and U.S. Army South (Panama). Commands located outside the United States are generally the Army component of DOD unified commands. In time of war or other national emergency, the organizations and units in these commands would become the advanced combat, combat support, and service elements of the Army.

Closer to home is the Army command charged with insuring the wartime readiness of the combat units located in the United States and certain possessions: the U.S. Army Forces Command (FORSCOM).

Forces Command is the largest of the major commands of the Army. It commands both active Army and Army Reserve units in forty-nine states (all states except Hawaii), in Puerto Rico, and in the Virgin Islands. Forces Command also supervises training for the Army National Guard units in the same geographic area; in a national emergency these Army National Guard units would also come under the command of FORSCOM. In the event of a full mobilization, under emergency conditions, FORSCOM could command nearly a million soldiers.

FORSCOM demonstrates the "One Army" concept that has transformed the Army in the past ten years or so. Each active Army, Army Reserve, and Army National Guard unit under the command of FORSCOM has been assigned a wartime mission that includes a proposed operational location and the relationship of the unit to other Army commands. Moreover, high-priority combat units in the reserve components of the Army have active-duty "partner" units that provide training support. Active-duty and reserve units of the same kind have the same organization, wear the same uniforms, and train with the same weapons and equipment. Having an assigned mission obviously helps provide a real sense of purpose to precombat training for these units.

FORSCOM has divided its geographical command into "armies" that also have defined areas. Five of these armies command the active Army and Army Reserve units assigned within their areas.

They also supervise the training of assigned National Guard units. A sixth group, designated the Third Army, has no assigned units. Instead, it is designed to be the headquarters of a rapid deployment force, under the command of the DOD unified command called CENTCOM. It, too, adheres to the "One Army" concept. Headquarters personnel include representatives from all three Army components, and units that may be assigned under emergency conditions include both Regular Army units and selected Army Reserve units.

ENLISTING IN THE ARMY

The Army requires about 130,000 new enlistees each year. Enlistments are for eight years, with active-duty options ranging from two to six years. The time remaining after completion of active duty must be spent in one of the reserve components, unless you choose to reenlist. Applicants must be American citizens or registered aliens between the ages of seventeen and thirty-four and in good health. Those wishing to enlist at age seventeen must have the approval of their parents or legal guardian.

Qualified high school graduates are able to choose training from among more than three hundred skills, clustered into twenty-nine career fields, as shown in the following table. Each of these fields has a well-defined career path leading to promotion and increased responsibility for those who elect to continue military service. Many of the specific military jobs have equivalent jobs in the civilian work force, in the event that you decide not to remain in the active Army.

New recruits are given a written guarantee for training in the chosen skill. In addition, as mentioned in Chapter IV, high school graduates who enlist for a designated military specialty can qualify for the Army College Fund and rapidly accumulate money, up to

LOCATION OF FORSCOM ARMIES AND MAJOR INSTALLATIONS

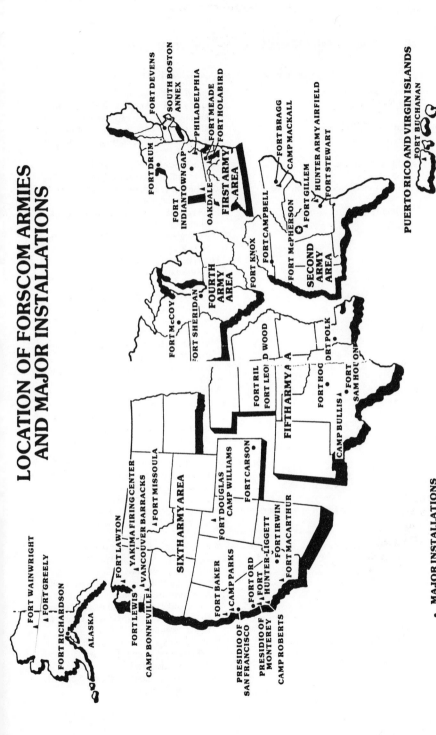

PUERTO RICO AND VIRGIN ISLANDS
FORT BUCHANAN

- MAJOR INSTALLATIONS
▲ SUB-INSTALLATIONS

ARMY ENLISTED CAREER FIELDS

Career Field	*General Qualifications Desired*
Administration	Courses in bookkeeping, typing, or office management; job experience.
Aviation Maintenance	Courses, work experience, or interest in mechanics, shop, math, electricity, and physics.
Air Defense Artillery	Aptitude for and experience in mechanical, electrical shop.
Air Defense Missile Maintenance	Aptitude for, experience in any mechanical or electrical area.
Ammunition	High school courses in chemistry, math, or electricity; job experience in excavation or construction; mechanical aptitude.
Armor	High degree of physical and mental coordination; mechanical aptitude; physical stamina.
Automatic Data Processing	Courses or experience in clerical areas, operation of office machines.
Aviation Communication Maintenance	Mechanical aptitude; interest in mechanics; background in physics, math, electricity; eligibility for security clearance.
Ballistic Missile Maintenance	Aptitude and interest in physics, math, electronics, mechanics.
Band	Musical background; audition required.
Chemical	Courses or work experience in chemistry, biology, electricity, mechanical shop, mechanical drawing or drafting.
Combat Engineering	Courses in carpentry, mechanical drawing, woodworking, shopwork, auto mechanics; mechanical aptitude; construction experience.
Communications: Electronics Maintenance	Interest in, aptitude for, courses in electricity or electronics.
Communications: Electronics Operations	Interest or experience in radio/TV/ electronics; security clearance may be required.
Cryptologic Operations	Aptitude for or studies in languages, geography, math, electronics; security clearance required.
Field Artillery	Mechanical aptitude; good physical and mental coordination.
Food Service	Interest and experience in restaurant and bakery work, or food stores; courses in home economics.
General Engineering	Interest or experience in any phase of construction or engineering; mechanical aptitude.
Infantry	Good physical and mental coordination; physical stamina.

Intercept Systems Maintenance	Courses, interest, or experience in physics, math, electricity, or electronics.
Law Enforcement	Experience in law enforcement or security work is helpful.
Mechanical Maintenance	Mechanical aptitude; interest in or courses in math, physics, shop, or mechanics.
Medical	Training in first aid or health sciences; experience as a medical or dental assistant helpful.
Military Intelligence	Courses in foreign languages, economics, geography, typing, and general office experience. A rigid character examination is given.
Petroleum	Courses in math, chemistry, and physical sciences are helpful.
Public Affairs and Audiovisual	Experience in communications, including radio, TV, writing, or photography; electricity or electronics helpful for some fields.
Supply and Service	Aptitude, interest, experience in clerical area, accounting, bookkeeping.
Topographic Engineering	Interest in or knowledge of drafting, mechanical drawing, math.
Transportation	Mechanical aptitude; experience with driving, operation of watercraft, auto mechanics.

$17,000, that could help pay for college education after separation from Army service. Other enlistees may qualify for bonuses of $1,500 to $5,000 by enlisting for, and completing training in, some skill areas in the combat arms (infantry, artillery, armor) or other designated skills. Bonuses up to $8,000 dollars may be paid other new enlistees, depending on the skill field and the Army's need for people in it.

Acceptance for any specific training depends, of course, on scores obtained on the Armed Services Vocational Aptitude Battery, the availability of openings in the skill field, and school quotas. Applicants for some specific skill options may be given separate qualification tests. Once accepted, however, otherwise qualified applicants may delay entrance on active duty for up to a year, under the Delayed Entry Program, awaiting a training opening.

Most recruits enter the Army in the lowest pay grade (E-1), but opportunities exist for enlistment at advanced pay grades. Applicants who have already acquired skills needed by the Army may be appointed to E-3 upon entry and promoted to E-4 after satisfactory performance in an Army job. If you have completed high school–

level training in skills needed by the Army, a similar program offers enlistment at the grade of E-2 or E-3 and a promise of promotion to E-4 after eight weeks' satisfactory performance in an Army unit. Similarly, graduates of two-year college courses, or those with sixty semester hours of college credit, particularly in some technical fields, may be qualified for appointment at E-3, with the prospect of accelerated promotion to E-4. Pay grades up to E-3 are also available to qualified graduates of Junior ROTC programs and to participants in Civil Air Patrol programs.

ARMY TRAINING

All new recruits are required to complete Army basic training, whatever the program under which they enlist. Basic training is designed to convert civilians into motivated and well-disciplined soldiers who are physically fit, qualified with a weapon, and drilled in the elements of soldiering.

Basic training lasts about eight weeks and is the same for both men and women. General purpose basic training centers are located at Fort Dix, New Jersey; Fort Jackson, South Carolina; Fort Knox, Kentucky; Fort Leonard Wood, Missouri; Fort McClellan, Alabama; and Fort Sill, Oklahoma.

Training for occupational specialties follows basic training, usually at another location. The Advanced Individual Training (AIT) varies in length depending upon the skill selected; the average time is about nine weeks. The AIT is designed to qualify the soldier to perform a job in a military unit; but the training does not end with graduation from a technical school. Thereafter, emphasis is on on-the-job training under the supervision of experienced soldiers and noncommissioned officers.

Initial entry training is somewhat different for soldiers who enlist for combat arms and combat support specialties. They receive both basic training and advanced training at the same installation, under a program called One Station Unit Training. Infantry soldiers are trained at the Infantry Center, Fort Benning, Georgia; armor training is given at the Armor Center, Ft. Knox; and soldiers designated for field artillery and air defense artillery train at Fort Bliss, Texas. One Station Unit Training is also given military police recruits (Ft. McClellan) and combat engineers (Ft. Leonard Wood).

Those who enlist for infantry, armor, artillery, or combat engineering specialties may join the Army's unique COHORT program. The COHORT program develops, from the first day of basic training, the teamwork essential to units in these fields.

Under the program, recruits are formed into COHORT companies during basic training, and they stay together for three years. After basic training, the COHORT company is assigned to an active Army division or other combat unit in the United States or overseas and undergoes unit training for about a year. Depending on circumstances, a COHORT unit assigned to a division or other combat unit in the United States may, after completion of unit training, be transferred to a division located in Europe or other overseas location.

Because of the nature of the COHORT program, the minimum enlistment time is three years plus training time (eleven to fourteen weeks). Reports from the field indicate that the program has been a great success, and the concept has been adopted for wider use. Participants in the program are also enthusiastic. Private Kevin Dane, from Los Angeles, California, described it this way: "You've got a strong bond between everybody, sort of like brothers." Squad leader Ron Gordon, from Wisconsin, put it another way: "These guys are really motivated. It's like a football team that's been together for years."

CARVING OUT A CAREER IN THE ARMY

You should recall from Chapter III that the Army expects its members to be concerned about job performance, to improve job skills, and, eventually, to advance to leadership or management positions. Performance evaluations, sometimes informal, begin when you enter the Army and never end while you are in the service.

Rewards for performance are also part of the Army system. During basic training, "Outstanding Recruit" may be the award to work toward. Later it will be "Outstanding Graduate of Class Such-and-Such" as you complete Advanced Individual Training. Then, on the job, perhaps "Driver of the Month." And so it goes. Work hard, study to improve your job performance, go out of your way sometimes to do something extra, suggest ways to improve the productivity of your section, seek responsibility: Someone will be watching you.

The promotion game begins shortly after basic training. An entry-level Private E-1 is usually promoted to Private E-2 within six months. Promotion to Private First Class (E-3) usually requires twelve months of active service, including four months in grade as an E-2, and the approval of the commanding officer. To be promoted to E-4, a soldier usually must have completed twenty-four months of active service, including at least six months as an E-3, and obtain the recommendation of his or her commander. At this level, quotas or other limitations on the number of promotions to E-4 may be imposed. In general, however, a conscientious soldier can expect to be promoted to E-4 within the first two years of service.

Naturally, there are exceptions to these standards. Those who enlist under programs that involve accelerated promotion, for example, do not follow the pattern. In general, moreover, a commanding officer may accelerate promotions to E-2, E-3, or to E-4 in exceptional cases. On the other hand, a commanding officer can also delay such promotions if the circumstances warrant.

In general, after some on-the-job training, you enter a period when you qualify for advanced schooling in your technical specialty. Those who enlisted for combat arms assignments, however, may be selected to attend a non-commissioned officer (NCO) academy where they develop leadership skills. Others in the combat arms may be able to volunteer for training in airborne or Ranger specializations. Qualified parachutists are usually assigned to airborne infantry divisions, though they may also qualify for duty with the elite Special Forces. Active "jumpers" also qualify for additional pay.

Promotion above the grade of E-4 can become intensely competitive. The number of promotions to grades E-5 through E-9 is controlled by the Department of the Army. Furthermore, the number of vacancies in a Military Occupational Specialty (MOS) varies from time to time; thus, the time in grade needed for promotion may also vary.

Eligibility for promotion to E-5 and E-6 is based on Skill Qualification Test scores for each MOS. Generally, a high school diploma (or a GED certificate) is also required. Once eligibility has been established, however, actual promotion depends upon the recommendation of a local command promotion board composed of officers and noncommissioned officers who examine the candidate in person.

At the level of E-5 to E-6, you usually complete some advanced schooling in your military specialty and can expect increasingly responsible assignments, starting as a squad or section leader and moving up to take charge of a platoon or a functional office. Your responsibilities become less specialized and require development of leadership and managerial talents. As your horizons expand, you may decide to enroll in courses given by a local college or a branch of a university; perhaps you will plot a course toward a college degree.

Perhaps, too, your expertise in your field will be such that you are selected to be an instructor at one of those schools where you were a student not too long ago. You may be able to attend an NCO academy or other special course devoted to management.

You may be appointed to a command advisory board or some

other official panel; you may even become a member of a promotion board and pass judgment on soldiers still on their way up the career ladder.

Long before you reach that stage, you will probably have had to wrestle with a decision about reenlisting. Handome bonuses are paid for reenlisting, but not to everyone. By the time your first enlistment is up, the Army will know whether you have the "stuff" for further useful service—and advancement. And so will you. The climb up the ladder from recruit may have been hard at times, but you are now a senior non-commissioned officer of the United States Army. You can relax a bit and smile to yourself: You are a professional.

Promotions to the grades of E-7 (Sergeant First Class), E-8 (First Sergeant/Master Sergeant), and E-9 (Sergeant Major, Command Sergeant Major, and Sergeant Major of the Army) are made at the Department of the Army. Promotion boards examine personnel records, performance reports, and other documents for each candidate and recommend promotion for those best qualified. Not everyone is promoted; but if you are, you can be sure that you have entered the executive ranks of the United States Army.

ARMY OFFICER CAREERS

The Army includes about 107,000 officers of all kinds, about one officer for every six enlisted men. About sixty-five percent of all commissioned officers on active duty are in the so-called company grades: Second Lieutenants, First Lieutenants, and Captains. This is the working part of the officer corps: the platoon commanders, junior staff officers, and company commanders. They are the most visible Army officers, usually the ones in direct contact with the enlisted personnel, and they often carry great responsibility. Company grade officers are also those most likely to leave the active Army, often to pursue civilian careers. As a result there is always plenty of room for newly commissioned officers.

Promotion above the rank of Captain is highly competitive, if only because only about thirty-five percent of all commissioned officers serve in higher grades. This, in turn, reflects the pyramidal structure of the officer corps and of the Army itself. Thus, promotion standards are tougher, and only the best-qualified officers are promoted to the field grades. As a rule, promotion to Major occurs during or before the eleventh year of active service. Promotion to Lt. Colonel now must be secured before or during the seventeeth year of service; if a Major is not promoted by that time, he is released from the Army.

The field grade officers account for most of the Army officers above the rank of Captain; they are comparable to middle-level business executives. Majors are often the staff officers in larger commands and headquarters; frequently they serve as executive officer in smaller commands or as chief of important departments of support installations and activities. Lieutenant Colonels are the commanders of most battalions (units with 500 to more than 1,000 personnel) and of the many installations and activities operated by the Army's technical and administrative services.

Field grade officers not only command, or control, large numbers of personnel, but they often are responsible for the management of complex Army programs and projects that have multimillion-dollar budgets. Attrition at this level is quite high, especially in time of peace, and only the best-qualified officers compete for further promotion, to the grade of Colonel. Promotion to Colonel normally occurs after about ten years in grade as a Lt. Colonel. Those who are not promoted may remain active until they have accumulated twenty-seven years' service; after that, they must retire.

Only about five percent of the Army's commissioned officers are Colonels and Generals, and all but about 400 officers at this level are Colonels. These are the senior executives and military managers. Among these officers is the small group of Generals who command the largest Army tactical units (divisions, corps, and armies), the Major Army Commands and their subcommands, and the administrative and technical branches of the Army. Other Generals are assigned to DOD unified commands in command or staff positions or to the Army General Staff.

HOW TO BECOME AN ARMY OFFICER

We have already explored two of the paths to commissioned status in the Army in Chapter IV: the United States Military Academy (West Point) and the Army Reserve Officers Training Corps (ROTC). Among the 9,150 newly commissioned officers who entered the Army during 1984, only about ten percent were graduates of the Military Academy, but nearly 60 percent were ROTC graduates, and that figure may have been greater during 1985 and 1986. Contrary to general opinion, many officers who received their commission through ROTC have risen to high-ranking positions in the Army, including several former Army Chiefs of Staff.

Army Reserve Officers Training Program (AROTC)

The Army Reserve Officers Training Program is a well-established method of producing young officers while they are attending colleges or universities of their choice. The Army offers this training at more than one thousand institutions, some of which are listed in Appendix D.

An advantage of ROTC is that it superimposes military training on the academic curriculum in such a way as to cause minimum disruption of the student's studies. In practice the program is divided into two two-year phases. Completion of both phases and graduation from college qualifies participants for a commission as Second Lieutenant. Honor graduates may be commissioned in the Regular Army; most ROTC graduates, however, receive commissions in the Army Reserve.

Students sign up for the first two-year phase of ROTC training during the normal registration session. No military obligation results from this Basic program. Students who wish to pursue the path to a commission compete for acceptance in the Advanced program, during the junior and senior college years. During this period, ROTC students receive a stipend of one hundred dolars a month; they also receive uniforms and necessary textbooks and course materials at no cost. Advanced ROTC students must attend a six-week Summer Camp.

Some students may qualify for the Advanced ROTC program without taking the first two years. These students are required to attend a six-week Basic camp before entering the program. Students with prior military service or with a Junior ROTC background may be excused from Basic camp.

Several thousand AROTC scholarships are available. The scholarships range from two to four years; they cover the costs of tuition, fees, and books; uniforms are provided free, and a stipend of one hundred dollars a month is paid each scholarship recipient for up to forty months during the four-year program. Courses of study must be approved by the Army.

High school seniors are encouraged to apply for the four-year scholarship no later than December first of the year before they intend to begin college studies. (See Appendix E.) Applications for shorter terms are accepted from students already enrolled in colleges and universities that host Army ROTC programs; the Professor of Military Science at the college can provide further information.

Direct Appointments

Direct commissioning of professionals from civilian life is widely used by the Army to recruit officers for the medical and health fields and for duty as chaplains. The Army also offers direct appointments to officer status to many others with training and experience in special fields. Some of the programs routinely offered are summarized below.

1. *Army Physicians.* Graduates of accredited medical schools or colleges of osteopathy who have completed internship and licensing requirements and who are engaged in the practice of medicine or surgery in the United States or one of its possessions are commissioned in the Army Reserve in a grade commensurate with experience. Normal entry grade is Captain or Major. Active-duty obligation: two years.

2. *Army Dentists.* Graduates of an accredited school in the United States, Puerto Rico, or Canada who are licensed to practice dentistry in the United States or one of its possessions are eligible for direct appointment in accordance with professional experience. Vacancies normally occur in the grades of Captain or Major. Service obligation: three years.

3. *Army Nurses.* Registered nurses who have graduated from an accredited nursing school with a Bachelor of Science in Nursing, not over thirty-three years of age, may be commissioned in the grade of Second Lieutenant to Major, depending on education and experience. Service obligation: three years.

4. *Army Veterinarians.* Graduates of accredited schools of veterinary medicine in the U.S. and Canada who are licensed to practice in the United States or one of its possessions, and who have not reached the age of thirty-three, may be commissioned in the Veterinary Corps, USArmy Reserve, in the grade of First Lieutenant or above, depending on professional qualifications. Age limit may be waived for candidates with prior service. Service obligation: three years.

5. *Occupational Therapists, Physical Therapists, and Dieticians.* United States citizens and resident aliens with a baccalaureate degree from an accredited college or university who are registered with the appropriate professional association may qualify for commissions ranging to Captain. Age limit: thirty-three. Service obligation: three years.

6. *Medical Specialists.* Professionals in fields allied to medicine who have a BA, BS, or graduate degree from an accredited school and who are under age thirty-five may be commissioned in grades up to Captain. Applicable fields: optometry, pharmacy, podiatry, audiology, psychology, medical laboratory sciences, entomology, sanitary engineering, social work, and hospital administration. Service obligation: three years.

7. *Physicians Assistants:* Graduates of a primary-care program of at least twenty months' duration, approved by the American Medical

Association, who are properly certified and physically qualified may be appointed Warrant Officer-1. Experience with military medicine is preferred. Service obligation: three years.

8. *Chaplains.* Members of the active clergy who hold a bachelor's degree (or equivalent) from an approved college or university and have completed a Master of Divinity degree or equivalent may be commissioned in the Army Reserve. Ecclesiastical endorsement required. Age limit: under forty. Service obligation: three years.

9. *Lawyers.* Graduates of an accredited law school who have been admitted to the bar of a federal court or the highest court in a state may be appointed First Lieutenant, Judge Advocate General Corps, USArmy Reserve. Age limits: twenty-one to thirty-three. Service obligation: three years.

10. *Army Professional and Technical Specialists.* Baccalaureate degree and related professional experience; qualify in testing program; must be capable of completing twenty years' service before age fifty-five. Commissioning grade depends on education and experience. Direct appointments depend on needs of the Army and may vary. Fields included: engineers, scientists, mathematicians, statisticians, business administrators, and others. Service obligation: three years.

Officer Candidate School (OCS)

College graduates under the age of twenty-nine may qualify for OCS training, provided they are United States citizens and meet the physical requirements. Generally, OCS is an enlistment option; that is, if you fail to complete OCS, you still have to serve out your enlistment in the Army (minimum of two years). Qualified enlisted persons and Warrant Officers already serving in the active Army may also apply for OCS training; in this case the requirement of a college degree is waived; however, a two-year college evaluation is made by the Army. This level can be reached through attendance at a junior college or by means of off-duty courses taken while in uniform. Active Army OCS graduates must serve on active duty for three years.

Army Warrant Officers

Army Warrant Officers perform duties much like those of commissioned officers, especially in the technical and administrative services, in law enforcement, and in military intelligence. More than 15,000 Warrant Officers served in the active Army in 1985.

Most Warrant Officers are appointed directly from the enlisted ranks, as vacancies occur. Appointees are required to attend a six-week Warrant Officer School. Warrant Officers wear the same uniforms as commissioned officers, but they have distinctive insignia of rank. Warrant Officer grades run from W-1 to W-4; pay at the W-1 level is about equal to that of a Second Lieutenant (0-1), and pay at W-4 is nearly that of a Major (0-4). Because Warrant Officers are highly qualified specialists or technicians, they are not subject to the same time-in-grade and other promotion criteria that govern officer careers. I recently read about a Chief Warrant Officer who retired at the age of sixty-two, for example, after more than forty-three years of Army service.

A program unique to the Army is the Warrant Officer Aviator Program, which trains helicopter pilots. This program can be entered from civilian life or after enlistment. In either case, applicants must meet rigid physical requirements and obtain a qualifying score on the Flight Aptitude Selection Test. Successful candidates attend a six-week Warrant Officer Military Development course before beginning the forty-week helicopter flight training course. Warrant Officer Aviators are obligated to serve on active duty for four years after completing flight training.

Other Commissioning Programs

The Army offers early commissioning programs for qualified medical, dental, osteopathic, veterinary, and theological students. Students, who must be college graduates, are commissioned in the Army Reserve but continue their studies. They may participate in Reserve training during summers between academic semesters, with full pay and allowances. When they graduate, they are promoted and enter active duty for three years.

BUILDING A CAREER IN THE ARMY

Each officer is assigned to an Army branch upon commissioning, and that branch supervises the officer's career development. Branch training begins with the basic officer's course, even for West Point graduates. Officers are then given initial assignments, often as platoon leaders with troop units or as junior managers in an administrative or technical facility.

Specialization for officers, except those in such fields as medicine, law, or religious affairs, has not always been a major concern of the Army. Recently, however, changes in the technological environment of the Army have fostered the development of some officer career fields that are neither branch-oriented nor branch-controlled. Other factors that favor the individual have also influenced officer career management. The result is a dual-specialty career management program under which all officers except those assigned to the Chaplain Corps, the Judge Advocate General Corps, and the Army Medical Department are expected to develop both a primary and an alternate career specialty.

Most specialties under this program remain branch-oriented; the others are administered by the Department of the Army without regard to the officer's branch affiliation. This approach allows officers to serve in any specialty for which they have appropriate skills or aptitude.

Branch affiliation is required, for example, for those who pursue the specialties designated as Infantry, Armor, Air Defense Artillery, or Field Artillery. On the other hand, a career officer of the Infantry (Specialty Code 11, Infantry) may have as an alternate specialty Foreign Area Officer (Specialty Code 48). Another Infantry officer may have the designated alternate specialty of Logistics Management (Specialty Code 70). Following are the Officer Career Specialty Codes and their titles.

Each career specialty is made up of a number of possible assignments that begin at the entry level (not always available to a

ARMY OFFICER CAREER SPECIALTIES

Specialty Title	Code
Air Defense Artillery	14
Armament Materiel Management	76
Armor	12
Atomic Energy	52
Automatic Data Processing	53
Aviation	15
Aviation Materiel Management	71
Chemical	74
Club Management	43
Combat Communications–Electronics	25
Communications–Electronics Engineering	27
Communications–Electronics Materiel Management	72
Comptroller	45
Counterintelligence/HUMINT	36
Education	47
Electronic Warfare/Cryptology	37
Engineer	21
Field Artillery	13
Finance	44
Fixed Telecommunications Systems	26

ARMY OFFICER CAREER SPECIALTIES (CONT'D)

Specialty Title	*Code*
Food Management	82
Foreign Area Officer	48
General Troop Support Materiel Management	83
Highway and Rail Operations	88
Infantry	11
Instructional Technology and Management	28
Law Enforcement	31
Logistics Management	70
Logistic Services Management	93
Maintenance Management	91
Marine and Terminal Operations	87
Missile Materiel Management	73
Munitions Materiel Management	75
Operations and Force Development	54
Operations Research/Systems Analysis	49
Personnel Administration and Administrative Management	42
Personnel Management	41
Petroleum Management	81
Procurement	97
Public Affairs	46
Research and Development	51
Supply Management	92
Tactical/Strategic Intelligence	35
Tank/Ground Mobility Materiel Management	77
Traffic Management	86
Transportation Management	95

Second Lieutenant) and become progressively more significant during the officer's career through the grade of Colonel. The system is flexible enough to accommodate officers who may be in the same specialty but who have different interests, abilities, and backgrounds (including civilian and military education).

Primary specialties are designated when an officer is commissioned; they are usually branch-oriented. An officer may, however, request another primary specialty at any time after completing two years' active commissioned service. Secondary specialties are normally designated by the time the officer has completed eight years of active duty. In some cases, a secondary specialty is designated much sooner, usually upon the achievement of some new status, such as completion of flight training or graduate-school training at a civilian university.

We may appear to be getting ahead of our story, since we have just brought you on active duty as a brand-new Second John. Already we can see stars in your eyes—the stars of a General, that is. So let us go back to the beginning.

No matter how you obtained your commission, your first assignment is to a basic branch course. Even officers who have received direct appointment in the Judge Advocate General Corps, the Chaplain Corps, or the various corps of the Army Medical Department are assigned to some military familiarization course.

Basic branch instruction gives you the background you need to function as an officer in a variety of assignments in your branch, generally into or through the grade of Captain. But the assignment you draw upon graduation from branch basic training will probably put you squarely on the bottom rung of the career ladder. This assignment, in fact, is know as a utilization tour: The Army reasoning is that it has to get something out of you after all that training. The climb to the top of the career ladder may seem long when you are standing on the bottom rung. So, keep your eyes on the stars: Even the Army Chief of Staff was once a Second Lieutenant.

It is never too early to learn what assignment options may be available in your primary specialty. Even if you have decided to stay in the Army only long enough to fulfill your service obligation, you may be able to improve your employment potential over the period of three or four years. Besides, the civilian job market may have changed by the time you have completed that obligation.

With a little homework you should be able to develop a course of action that will keep you on a steady upward career path. Begin to think about an alternate specialty; you might be able to work into something you had not even thought possible. If you have already given it some thought, check to be sure you are on the right track.

Find out about the Army schools or civilian university programs (graduate studies) that can give you a boost up the career ladder or enhance your planned civilian career. Be sure you understand the eligibility requirements and the timing. For example, attendance at your branch Advanced Officer Course is probably a must in career planning, but that may be a few years down the road. Meanwhile, there is also a wide choice of short courses in various fields related to your job or career interests. Find out how to take advantage of those opportunities.

Finally, the more interest you show in the Army, the more interest the Army will show in you. Your career as an officer is not assured just because someone pinned bars on your uniform.

Chapter VI

The United States Navy

The United States Navy, like the Army, has a proud tradition that reaches back to the days of the American Revolution. Also like the Army, the Navy continues to honor its heroes.

John Paul Jones, daring captain of the *Ranger* and, later, the *Bonhomme Richard*, for example, carried the spirit of the rebelling colonials into British waters and even onto British soil with raids along the English coast. Stephen Decatur, son of a Revolutionary War privateer and naval officer, and already known for his bold exploits in the war with Tripoli (1801–1805), added to his fame by forcing a treaty on the Pasha of Algeria and securing payment from the Pashas of Tunis and Tripoli for injury to Americans and damage to American ships and cargoes. The treaty, concluded in 1815, ended the long, expensive, and sometimes bloody history of interference with American and other commercial shipping along the coast of North Africa.

Then there were the brothers Perry. One, Oliver Hazard Perry, won a vicious naval battle on Lake Erie during the War of 1812 that reinforced American claims to the old Northwest Territory. The battle flag of Perry's flagship bore the famous motto, "Don't Give Up the Ship!" When the battle ended with the surrender of the British, Perry sent an equally brief message to his commander: "We have met the enemy, and they are ours."

Matthew C. Perry, the other brother, is best remembered for his mission to Japan in 1853–54, under the authority of the U.S. Department of State, during which he negotiated the treaty that opened Japan to trade with the West. But Matthew Perry is perhaps better remembered in Navy lore because of his roles in the creation of the Naval Academy at Annapolis, Maryland, the founding of the Navy's engineering corps (the modern Seabees), the inauguration of scientific naval gunfire training, and the conversion of the Navy from sailing vessels to steam-powered ships. Indeed, Matthew Perry is sometimes known as the father of the steam navy.

David Glasgow Farragut, a Tennesseean who sided with the Union at the start of the Civil War, became an Admiral of the Navy with a reputation rivaling that of England's famous Lord Nelson. "Damn the torpedoes," Farragut is supposed to have shouted as he led his fleet against the harbor defenses at Mobile Bay at the start of what was to be a decisive naval action of the war. But Farragut also served in the Mediterranean, helped suppress pirates in the West Indies, and carried out a mission to Mexico to protect the lives and property of Americans stranded there during the Franco-Mexican War. In the mid-1850s, Farragut was in charge of the construction of the Mare Island Naval Yard, an important move that later helped project American naval power into the Pacific Ocean basin.

Another nineteenth-century officer may have had a greater influence on the development of the modern U.S. Navy than any other single American, despite his somewhat routine career of shore and sea duty. Captain Alfred Thayer Mahan's influence was due more to the power of his pen than to that of his officer's saber. Mahan lectured on naval tactics, strategy, and history at the Naval War College in the mid-1880s. Two books he wrote based on those lectures revolutionized naval strategy. His main argument was that the nation that controlled the seas, and denied their use to the enemy, also controlled the key factor in warfare.

Those theories were more than adequately tested during the Spanish-American War; indeed, Mahan was then a consultant to the Secretary of the Navy. In July 1898, a large Navy force under Admiral William T. Sampson outgunned the Spanish fleet off the coast of Cuba. The defeat of the Spanish also forced the surrender of the large Spanish Army garrison at Santiago de Cuba and virtually ended the war.

More important for the future of the U.S. Navy, by far, was the American victory in another naval battle that had already taken place far away in the Pacific Ocean: the Battle of Manila Bay. Commodore George Dewey, commanding the Navy's new Asiatic Squadron, steamed away from his base in China in search of a Spanish naval squadron. Finding the Spanish at anchor in Manila Bay, he attacked and destroyed the squadron on May 1, 1898. A few months later, after the arrival of an Army expeditionary force, the Asiatic Squadron was instrumental in securing the surrender of Manila itself. Dewey's victory in the Philippines confirmed the growing role of the United States in the Pacific Ocean. The United States Navy has played a leading part there ever since.

There are many more such examples of Navy heroes, and not a few of Navy scholars. But the legacy of John Paul Jones, Stephen Decatur, the Perrys, Farragut, Mahan, Sampson, and Dewey should help us to understand better the role of the modern U.S. Navy among the military services of the United States.

MISSIONS AND ORGANIZATION OF THE NAVY

The Navy can trace its history to October 13, 1775, when the Continental Congress authorized the commissioning of two small ships for what soon became the Navy of the United Colonies. In the two hundred years since that time, the Navy has become a major, technologically advanced force dedicated to the protection of the United States, its interests, and its citizens around the globe. The several aspects of the mission of today's Navy are, nevertheless, both rooted in historical tradition and responsive to the expanded role of the United States as a world power.

The Navy is, in the first place, organized for combat at sea. This aspect of its mission means that our naval forces are designed to seek out and destroy enemy naval forces, to prevent them from interfering with commerce at sea, and to protect vital military supply lines. The Navy has kept pace with and often been ahead of advancing military technology. Naval forces now use land- and carrier-based aircraft of all descriptions, aircraft carriers powered by nuclear energy, long-range nuclear-powered submarines, missiles, and even satellites to support this mission.

Another important part of the Navy mission is to support military operations on land, most notably operations that require American or allied ground forces to land on hostile shores. These ground forces are usually provided by the Army, but the Navy may also use its own ground force, the United States Marines. For the purposes of this book, the Marine Corps is treated as a separate military service, in Chapter VII.

In addition to those aspects of the Navy mission that serve to give it combat superiority at sea, the Navy also carries out a strategic mission that requires a high, continual state of operational readiness: the prompt employment of ship-based intercontinental ballistic missiles should the mainland of the United States be attacked by a major foreign power. This mission involves the worldwide deployment of nuclear-powered submarines equipped to fire such missiles, thus augmenting other strategic deterrence capabilities like those of the Strategic Air Command. The submarines can cruise unsupported for great distances away from their home bases; they often operate submerged for long periods of time. The mission is coordinated at the top level of the Department of Defense, but the crews of the submarines are specially trained Navy volunteers.

A Navy enlisted man striking for the rating of Boilerman while working in the engineroom of a cargo ship.

Of course, the Navy has other missions that keep it busy. For example, in time of war or other emergency Navy ships and crews have traditionally helped protect the lives and property of citizens who live and work outside the United States. The Navy has often been concerned with humanitarian projects. In recent years, for example, U.S. Navy ships rescued thousands of Vietnamese "boat people" from certain death at sea. The Navy is also constantly "showing the flag" during goodwill visits to foreign ports as part of the overall diplomatic effort of the United States.

From another point of view, Navy units and individual Navy officers have always engaged in explorations of the seven seas and the lands that border them. Young Oliver Hazard Perry died during an expedition to explore the Orinoco River. A U.S. Navy engineer, Robert Edwin Peary, led the first expedition to the North Pole. Richard Evelyn Byrd, a Navy aviator, was the first to fly over the North Pole; his later explorations of the Antarctic region set the stage for the scientific study of that area that continues today, under U.S. Navy auspices.

Probably the most important peacetime Navy mission remains that of protecting seaborne commerce and guaranteeing free passage of international waterways, or "freedom of navigation." During the eighteenth and nineteenth centuries, the Navy waged long campaigns against the Caribbean pirates. Today's Navy is still concerned about pirates, in other parts of the world far from the American mainland: in the Straits of Molucca, for example. At other times, the Navy has been used to force foreign governments to comply with international laws concerning freedom of navigation.

Organization of the United States Navy

The organization of the United States Navy includes the operating forces, mostly at sea or ready to go to sea, and the shore establishment required to support them. The Department of the Navy, in Washington, D.C., controls or coordinates both the operating forces and the shore establishment.

The Secretary of the Navy, a civilian, is appointed by the President of the United States, but he is responsible to the Secretary of Defense for the day-to-day operation of the Navy. The Secretary of the Navy is responsible for planning and coordinating the use of merchant shipping to support the Navy in time of war; he also supervises the so-called mothball fleet of deactivated cargo and other ships. In time of war, also, the Secretary of the Navy is responsible for the management and operation of the U.S. Coast Guard.

The senior Navy Admiral and the principal military adviser to the Secretary of the Navy is the Chief of Naval Operations. This officer is equivalent to the Chief of Staff of the Army or Air Force; he is the Navy's representative to the Joint Chiefs of Staff, the Department of Defense coordinating organization.

A Navy woman qualifies for the rating of Equipment Operator Constructionman in a construction battalion.

The Chief of Naval Operations presides over a military staff that assists him in meeting his responsibilities for planning and carrying out most aspects of Navy operations. A Vice Chief and several Deputy Chiefs of Naval Operations and Directors on this staff carry out designated functions that include administration, personnel policies and procedures, intelligence and security, military plans and operations, education and training, research and development, procurement and supply of naval equipment, Navy Reserve affairs, and medical programs and facilities.

The principal operating forces of the United States Navy are the fleets and other naval commands shown below, with their naval forces (in parentheses) and the location of their headquarters. Some of these forces are components of unified commands under the operational control of the Department of Defense, such as CINCPAC (Seventh Fleet) and CINCEUR (Sixth Fleet).

Atlantic Fleet (Second Fleet)	Norfolk, Virginia
Military Sealift Command	Washington, D.C.
Mine Warfare Command	Charleston, S.C.
Naval Forces Central Command (Middle East Force)	Pearl Harbor, Hawaii
Naval Forces Europe (Sixth Fleet)	London, England
Naval Forces Southern Command	Rodman, Panama
Pacific Fleet (Third Fleet, Seventh Fleet)	Pearl Harbor, Hawaii

The naval forces in these commands are not rigidly structured like the combat forces of the ground forces. For example, the number and kinds of ships assigned to the Sixth Fleet, which operates in the Mediterranean Sea, varies from time to time. In fact, the ships and their crews rotate about every six months. The Sixth Fleet is a permanent command, nevertheless, with an Admiral, a permanent flagship, a staff, and assigned bases.

Furthermore, combatant ships assigned to a naval command at a given time are usually organized into temporary task forces for specific operational or training missions. The nucleus of a task force may be a battleship, a cruiser, or an aircraft carrier, depending on the mission. Auxiliary or noncombatant ships such fuel tankers, supply ships, repair ships, and ammunition ships may also be assigned to task forces; or they may operate in general support of the fleet or other Navy combat command.

A portion of the Navy's operating forces is also assigned to two shore-based commands: the Atlantic Sea Frontier and the Pacific Sea Frontier. They are responsible for the defense of the continental United States and its territories and the protection of commercial shipping. The interior of the United States is divided into Naval Districts that command or supervise U.S. Navy shore installations and activities within their jurisdiction.

The reserve forces of the U.S. Navy, about 195,000 strong, are organized as part of the total Navy, with assigned wartime missions.

Most of these missions are designed to support the combat forces of the Navy rather than to augment them, as is the case with the Army. The Navy Reserve units account for almost all the Navy's wartime logistic support (airlift and sealift), cargo handling, shipping control, combat search and rescue, and minesweeping capabilities. The Reserves also provide about two-thirds of the Navy construction battalions (Seabees) to the total Navy force under wartime conditions. Combat forces, including carrier air units and combatant surface ships, exist in the Navy Reserve; but they would contribute only marginally to augmentation of the combat capabilities of the active Navy.

The Navy Around the World

The size and disposition of American naval forces have changed over the past century to match the expanding power of the United States around the world. Today's Navy comprises more than 490 thousand enlisted men and women and nearly 69,000 officers. The 560 thousand members of the active Navy operate more than 550 ships and about 6,000 airplanes. In 1985 almost forty percent of everyone in the Navy was reported to be "afloat," that is, serving aboard Navy ships around the world. Another ten percent of its total strength, about 56,500 men and women, served ashore at locations outside the continental United States. "Join the Navy and See the World" was the Navy recruiting slogan for many years, and it still applies.

The remaining fifty percent of the men and women in the Navy serve in the continental United States, largely in the shore establishment that supports the operating forces. The shore establishment consists of seventeen functional organizations known variously as bureaus, commands, offices, and services. They support the Navy as a whole in fields already mentioned and a few more: personnel, communications, intelligence and security, medical affairs, legal services, criminal investigation, education and training, supplies, engineering, oceanography, and automatic data processing. The Navy also has several systems commands concerned with various aspects of naval air systems, naval sea systems, and space and naval warfare systems.

ENLISTING IN THE NAVY

The Navy needs about 95,000 new enlisted personnel each year to fill job vacancies. Initial enlistment is usually four years, but shorter and longer terms are available. Men and women between the ages of seventeen and thirty-four may apply; those of age seventeen must have the permission of their parents or legal guardian. Applicants must be physically qualified, U.S. citizens or resident aliens, free of any criminal record, and qualified or able to qualify on the Armed Services Vocational Aptitude Battery (ASVAB). Both men and women may be married, but married enlistees may experience many strains on their marriage during the early stages of Navy training.

Civilian education can be extremely important to anyone considering enlisting in the Navy. Many Navy training programs require that enlistees be high school graduates. However, new enlistees who have not yet graduated may be given up to 365 days to complete high school (or obtain a GED) under the Delayed Entry Program. The program guarantees training in the skill field for which they qualified when they enlisted. Advanced civilian vocational or technical training, or successful completion of some college study can qualify recruits for enlistment in advanced pay grades, up to E-3 or Seaman.

Enlistees who have completed an accredited Junior Naval Reserve Officers Training (JNROTC) or who served in the Sea Cadets may also be eligible for an advanced pay grade, up to E-3.

Navy Enlisted Career Fields

The Navy offers enlistees training in about sixty of the seventy or so career fields or ratings available in the Navy. These ratings are grouped in the ten categories shown in the table below. Each career field is structured to permit the person to progress from entry-level job to supervisory position during a normal Navy career.

Navy ratings often have titles different from the Military Occupations listed in Chapter III. They are, in fact, usually clusters of those occupations. Military Occupations that may be included in each rating are given in parentheses.

Most of these career fields are available to both men and women. The exceptions for women are ratings designated as combat specialties. On the other hand, women serve aboard auxiliary (or noncombatant) ships, in certain aviation units, and, for a maximum of six months, on board any Navy ship that is not expected to be engaged in combat operations during that duty period. These provisions make it possible for Navy enlisted women to be more fully competitive with enlisted men in their chosen career fields.

An example or two may help to illustrate this trend toward widening career opportunities for women in the Navy. Recently, the Navy announced the assignment of the first woman to become a

NAVY ENLISTED CAREER FIELDS

1. Administrative and Clerical Group
   Cryptologic Technician (Intelligence Specialist, Electronic Instrument Repairer, Precision Instrument Repairer)
   Data Processing Technician (Computer Operator, Data Entry Specialist, DP Equipment Repairer)
   Disbursing Clerk (Payroll Specialist, Accounting Specialist)
   Intelligence Specialist (Intelligence Specialist)
   Journalist (Reporter and Newswriter)
   Legalman (Legal Technician, Court Reporter)
   Mess Management Specialist (Food Service Specialist)
   Navy Counselor (Caseworker and Counselor)
   Personnelman (Personnel Specialist)
   Postal Clerk (Postal Specialist)
   Radioman (Radio Operator, Radio Intelligence Operator, Radio Equipment Repairer)
   Religious Program Specialist (Religious Program Specialist)
   Ships Serviceman (Sales and Stock Specialist, Barber)
   Storekeeper (Stock and Inventory Specialist)
   Yeoman (Administrative Support Specialist, Secretary/Stenographer, Lodging Specialist)

2. Aviation Group
   Aerographers Mate (Weather Observer)
   Aircrew Survival Equipmentman (Survival Equipment Specialist)
   Air Traffic Controller (Air Traffic Controller)
   Aviation Anti-Submarine Warfare Operator (Radar/Sonar Operator)
   Aviation Anti-Submarine Warfare Technician (Electronic Weapons Systems Repairer)
   Aviation Boatswain's Mate (Air Crew Member)
   Aviation Electricians Mate (Aircraft Electrician)
   Aviation Electronics Technician (Electronic Instrument Repairer)
   Aviation Fire Control Technician (Electronic Weapons Systems Repairer, Radar/Sonar Operator)
   Aviation Machinists Mate (Air Crew Member, Aircraft Mechanic, Heating and Cooling Mechanic)
   Aviation Ordnance Man (Air Crew Member, Ordnance Mechanic)
   Aviation Maintenance Administration Man (Maintenance Data Analyst)
   Aviation Storekeeper (Stock and Inventory Specialist)
   Aviation Structural Mechanic (Aircraft Mechanic)
   Aviation Support Equipment Technician (Aircraft Launch and Recovery Specialist)
   Photographers Mate (Photographer, Motion Picture Camera Operator, Photographic Equipment Repairer)

3. Construction Group
   Builder (Carpenter)
   Construction Electrician (Building Electrician)
   Construction Mechanic (Automobile Mechanic, Heavy Equipment Mechanic, Powerhouse Mechanic)
   Engineering Aide (Surveying Technician)
   Equipment Operator (Construction Equipment Operator, Paving Equipment Operator)

NAVY ENLISTED CAREER FIELDS (CONT'D)

3. Construction Group (cont'd)
   Steelworker (Ironworker, Rigger, Welder)
   Utilitiesman (Plumber and Pipefitter, Water and Sewage Teatment Plant
      Operator, Heating and Cooling Mechanic)
4. Deck Group
   Boatswains Mate (Seaman, Boat Operator)
   Electronic Warfare Technician (Electronic Weapons Systems Repairer,
      Radar/Sonar Operator)
   Master-at-Arms (Military Police, Detective)
   Ocean Systems Technician (Weather Observer–Oceanographer Assistant,
      Electronic Technician)
   Operations Specialist (Radar and Sonar Operator)
   Quartermaster (Quartermaster)
   Sonar Technician (Radar/Sonar Operator, Electronic Weapons System
      Repairer)
   Signalman (Radio Operator, Telephone Operator, Teletype Operator)
5. Dental Group
   Dental Technician (Dental Specialist, Radiologic Technician, Dental
      Laboratory Technician)
6. Electronics and Precision Instrument Group
   Data Systems Technician (Data Processing Equipment Repairer)
   Electronics Technician (Electronic Instrument Repairer)
   Instrumentman (Precision Instrument Repairer)
   Opticalman (Precision Instrument Repairer)
7. Engineering and Hull Group
   Boiler Technician (Boiler Technician, Powerplant Operator)
   Electricians Mate (Ship Electrician, Electrical Product Repairer, Power Plant
      Electrician)
   Engineman (Marine Engine Mechanic; operates ship's proplusion equipment)
   Gas Turbine Systems Technician
   Hull Maintenance Technician (Shipfitter, Welder, Sheet Metal Worker)
   Interior Communications Electrician (Telephone Technician, Line
      Installer/Repairer)
   Machinery Repairman (Marine Engine Repairman, Machinist)
   Machinists Mate (Marine Engine Mechanic, Heating and Cooling Mechanic)
   Molder (Machinist)
   Patternmaker (Carpenter)
8. Medical Group
   Hospital Corpsman (Medical Service Technician, various health care
      occupations, except Dental)
9. Miscellaneous Group
   Illustrator-Draftsman (Drafter, Graphic Designer, and Illustrator)
   Lithographer (Printing Specialist)
10. Ordnance Group
    Fire Control Technician (Radar and Sonar Operator, Electronic Weapons
       Systems Repairer)
    Gunner's Mate (Artillery Crew Member)
    Mineman (Artillery Crew Member, Ordnance Mechanic)
    Missile Technician (Artillery Crew Member, Ordnance Mechanic)

construction equipment operator. A few years ago, I had an opportunity to watch a woman member of a Navy aviation unit as she expertly brought a flight of screaming jet fighters into the aircraft parking area at the Naval Air Station at Guantanamo Bay, Cuba. She seemed completely at ease as she supervised the placement of wheel chocks, and she had a smile on her face as she gave each pilot the "All clear." Maybe not every woman who enlists in the Navy would be excited about either of those jobs. The point is, however, that they have the choice.

New enlistees can usually select training in a rating of their choice during preenlistment processing, and about seventy-five percent do so. Confirmation of training in that career field depends to a great extent upon scores attained on the ASVAB and, in some cases, upon physical qualifications. New enlistees can also expect a review of the selected training option during their basic training; final classification takes place at that time.

Those who are undecided or who have not qualified for a skill of their choice enter the Navy's apprenticeship program. This program stresses development of technical skills through on-the-job training instead of classroom study. It is not a program for "leftovers," however. Rather it offers enlistees a group of possible career fields that is the largest in the Navy. Those who enter the apprenticeship program must enlist for four years, but they are often able to sample several job fields before choosing a specialty. In general terms, training is available as seamen (deck department trades), firemen (engineering trades), and airmen (naval aviation trades). *Subfarer*, a special apprenticeship program, trains men to serve aboard submarines.

The Navy apprenticeship program is not to be confused with the joint agreement between the Department of Labor and the Navy that develops apprentices in specific trades (see Appendix C).

Three Navy programs offer qualified high school graduates opportunities to train in critical technological fields: nuclear energy, advanced electronics, and other advanced fields that include medical specialties, operation and maintenance of gas turbine engines, and electronic equipment repair. Training in these programs may require up to two years of serious study, but promotions are accelerated for successful candidates. Special bonuses are also paid during or after the training in some cases; handsome reenlistment bonuses may also be paid to fully qualified personnel in some of these fields. Because of the extensive training involved, candidates are required to enlist for six years. Candidates for the nuclear energy field must not have reached their twenty-fifth birthday on the date of enlistment.

The Navy provides extra pay for sea duty, submarine duty, diving duty, demolitions duty, duty as a crew member of an aviation team, for certain ratings that require special training, and for duty in combat zones.

Training for a Navy Rating

All new Navy enlistees are required to complete recruit or boot training before they receive advanced training in a specialty. Recruit training lasts about eight weeks and is designed to prepare young civilians for life in the Navy. All recruit training is conducted at the three Naval Training Centers, at Orlando, Florida; San Diego, California; and Great Lakes, Illinois (near Chicago). Men may be assigned to any of the three centers; women are trained only at Orlando.

Wherever you may be assigned, the training is much the same. You receive lectures on Navy history, traditions, and customs, instruction in basic military subjects, and technical training peculiar to the Navy. Physical conditioning and competitive sports are emphasized. During boot camp, training begins at 5:30 am. and lasts until 9:30 pm. The evening schedule may become more relaxed toward the end of the training, but no leave time is allowed recruits until they have completed boot training.

Specialty training follows the completion of basic training. Those who elected training at a technical school may remain at the same Naval Training Center, but they are transferred to a Class A School operated by the Service School Command. Others may be reassigned to attend courses at one of the other hundred or so technical schools in the Navy's education and training system. The lengths of these courses vary.

After completion of initial technical training, you will probably be assigned to a job aboard a ship or at a shore installation. There you will gain additional on-the-job training under the supervision of experienced Petty Officers.

Apprenticeship candidates are assigned to a four-week course designed to further the technical skills they acquired during recruit training. Apprentices are then ordered to the Fleet for duty and on-the-job training.

In either case, training does not end with graduation from the Class A school or the apprenticeship orientation course. The Navy system requires continued study related to your rate, either by correspondence courses or by attendance at advanced training courses.

Enlistment in the Navy in no way is an end in itself. Career development opportunities are abundant and varied within the rating system. They include procedures for acquiring highly specialized skills within a rating, for assignment in general fields outside a rating, and for moving from one rating field to another. Moreover, the Navy has several commissioning programs for qualified enlisted personnel. These are discussed under the heading Officer Careers in the Navy.

Advancement in the Navy

Most new enlistees enter the Navy as Seaman Recruits (E-1), but, as in the other military services, the promotion game begins as soon as recruit training has been completed. In a sense, the scramble for promotion may begin even during recruit training: Exceptional recruits may be promoted to E-2 upon graduation. Promotion to Apprentice Seaman (E-2) normally occurs upon the completion of six months of active duty, however, provided the candidate is recommended by the commanding officer.

Promotion beyond pay grade E-2 is based on a number of factors, including job performance, grades on competitive examinations, recommendations of supervisors, time spent in the present grade, and total length of service. Although each job in a career field has a defined path leading to supervisory positions, it is not possible to predict when promotions will occur.

In general, however, promotion to E-3 requires six months in grade as an E-2 (Apprentice Seaman), successful completion of a correspondence course designed to improve general military proficiency, demonstration of professional competence in the specialty, and the recommendation of the commanding officer.

These general rules are, of course, subject to exceptions. Men and women who enlist for an advanced technical program, in particular in the electronics and nuclear energy fields, may be advanced more rapidly. Others may also enter the Navy with pay grades up to E-3 (Seaman), as already noted.

Advancement to Petty Officer ratings in the Navy (E-4 through E-6) is usually based on a composite score or multiple determined for each individual. The calculation includes points earned for awards, advanced schooling (including correspondence courses), time in grade, military and professional proficiency, and scores on Navy-wide competitive examinations for the rate. A satisfactory grade on a competitive, Navy-wide examination of general military proficiency is required for promotion to E-4 (Petty Officer Third Class) and E-5 (Petty Officer Second Class). With all this in hand, the recommendation of the candidate's commanding officer must also be favorable. Once all the requirements for advancement have been met, promotions are made as vacancies occur in the career field; the candidate who has achieved the highest multiple is promoted first.

The Navy's promotion scheme results in fierce competition at times. The reenlistment rate for first-term enlisted men and women is very high, about 60 percent; but the reenlistment rate for career Navy men and women is the lowest for the military services: about 80 percent. On the other hand, reenlistment in the Navy at the petty officer level is not entirely voluntary. The Navy may simply reject anyone who has not performed according to expectations. The low figure for career reenlistments, therefore, seems to reflect the Navy-wide competition for promotion to senior petty officer ratings. By the same reasoning, it suggests a high level of military and professional competence among the senior enlisted members of the Navy: All have met very tough standards for promotion.

Promotions to E-7 (Chief Petty Officer) and above are made by the Department of the Navy, based on review of individual personnel files and the recommendation of a promotion board. The road to the top can be a difficult one, requiring a great deal of hard work and study. But the rank of Chief Petty Officer in the Navy has traditionally been without parallel among the military services of the United States.

OFFICER CAREERS IN THE NAVY

Naval officers are a varied breed despite the fact that they all wear the same uniform. Naval tradition favors those who will eventually command ships: the surface warfare officers, the submarine warfare officers, and even the naval aviators. But many other officers are specialists in these days of the high-tech Navy. Under the circumstances, the officer corps of the Navy is divided into three categories: unrestricted line officers, restricted line officers, and staff corps officers.

Unrestricted line officers are not restricted to the performance of duties in one field. This group includes the surface warfare officers, submarine warfare officers, naval aviators, and naval flight officers, along with some who do specialize at one time or another: nuclear power instructors, special operations officers, and special warfare officers. The special operations officers are men and women who volunteer in such areas as diving and salvage and explosive ordnance disposal. Special warfare officers, all men, lead the sea-air-land (SEAL) teams that may operate behind enemy lines. The final group in this category are the general unrestricted line officers. They are specialists in communications, space operations, engineering, political-military affairs, training, management analysis. and other areas. These officers may command most types of shore activity.

Restricted line officers perform duties only in their area of expertise. Their specialties include various engineering fields, oceanography, intelligence, public affairs, and cryptology.

Staff corps officers are those assigned to one of the eight Navy corps: Chaplain Corps, Civil Engineer Corps, Dental Corps, Judge Advocate General Corps, Medical Corps (physicians), Medical Service Corps (health care specialists), Nurse Corps, and Supply Corps. Staff Corps officers are obviously highly qualified specialists. Most, but not all, serve ashore, in support of the Navy's operating forces.

At first glance the division between line and staff officers may appear rigid, perhaps unfair. However, it permits Navy officers to build a career in the specialization in which they are most interested, and for which they are best qualified. This, in turn, helps the Navy to attract the specialists it needs.

Officer ranks in the Navy differ from those in the ground forces. Entry-level officers are called Ensigns and are in the first officer pay grade, 0-1 (see Appendix B). Ensigns are promoted to Lieutenant Junior Grade (0-2) and in turn to Lieutenant (0-3). About 60 percent of all Navy commissioned officers serve in these three grades.

Many of these junior officers are serving on obligated tours of duty, as Naval Reserve officers or in accordance with various obligations growing out of Navy-supported training. Many also leave the Navy when their obligation is met and return to civilian life.

The well-qualified Navy officer should be promoted to Lieutenant within the first five years of active duty. Up to that grade, promotions are relatively routine, on a fully qualified basis. Officer career development really starts at the level of Lieutenant. Assignments are more challenging, a subspecialty is developed, and opportunities are offered for advanced training at Navy service schools or in civilian universities. Outstanding officers may be assigned to attend the Navy staff college.

Promotion above the rank of Lieutenant depends to a great extent upon the individual, but the process is increasingly competitive. Promotion to Lieutenant Commander (0-4), Commander (0-5), and Captain (0-6) is made on a best-qualified basis. Job performance, military and civilian educational qualifications, and command or management potential are all taken into consideration, along with time in grade, total length of service, and other factors. As in the other military services, the objective is to have an all-career Navy after the eleventh or twelfth year of service. Lieutenants should be promoted to Lt. Commander (0-4) by their eleventh year on duty. Promotion to Commander should come about six years later. Along the way come assignments to advanced service schools such as the Armed Forces Staff College or, perhaps, the Naval War College for exceptional officers.

The Navy has another category of officer: the Warrant Officer. Most Warrant Officers are highly qualified career specialists. In general, they are selected from among the senior enlisted ranks. Navy Warrant Officers perform at four levels; their pay grades run from W-1 to W-4, which roughly equal pay grades 0-1 to 0-4 for commissioned officers. Warrant Officers wear the same uniforms as commissioned officers but have different rank and sleeve insignia.

Becoming a Navy Officer

The paths to a career as a Navy Officer are much the same as those of the other military services. Graduates of Officer Candidate Schools and other commissioning programs for enlisted men and women amounted to nearly two fifths of the 5,344 newly commissioned officers who entered active Navy service in 1984. Naval ROTC graduates made up another one fifth of the total. The other two fifths were mostly graduates of the U.S. Naval Academy (fifteen percent of the total), direct appointments (sixteen percent), and graduates of the Health Professions Scholarship Program (eight percent). What this adds up to is that about six other commissioned officers entered the Navy in 1984 for every graduate of the Naval Academy.

Competing for an appointment to Annapolis may be just the thing for you, but there are many other ways to earn a Navy commission, if that is your goal and you are between the ages of nineteen and twenty-nine (slightly younger for some fields), a citizen of the United States, and physically qualified.

In general, a college degree is the essential first step toward a Navy commission. If you are planning to go to college or are already in college, probably the best way to earn your commission is through the Naval ROTC Scholarship Program. Graduates of this program earn commissions in the Regular Navy and generally become unrestricted line officers or Naval Aviators. You may wish to refer to Chapter IV for more details.

Another approach is to attend Naval Officer Candidate School after you have obtained your degree. Depending upon your interests and qualifications, you can train for a line commission, a staff corps commission, or a commission in naval aviation or nuclear propulsion. In most cases, you should apply for these programs during your junior year of college. Successful graduates receive commissions in the Naval Reserve; they are obligated to serve on active duty for varying numbers of years, up to seven, depending upon the training option.

If you plan to go on to graduate school to become a physician, a dentist, a lawyer, or a theologian, you should not overlook the several Navy programs that offer you a commission when you graduate, usually at an advanced grade. Most of these programs help you meet your academic expenses.

The Armed Forces Health Professions Scholarship Program can, in fact, provide up to four years of fully paid medical schooling for qualified students. Applicants must already be enrolled in, or accepted by, an accredited medical or osteopathy school. Under the scholarship program, students also receive a monthly allowance for expenses. Graduates are commissioned in the Navy Medical Corps or Medical Service Corps.

The Navy Dental Student Program offers salaried clerkships at Navy health care facilities; graduates are commissioned Navy Dental Officers and go on active duty.

The Navy has a similar clerkship program for law students; upon graduation, they go into the Navy as full-time lawyers with the Judge Advocate General's Corps.

If you are contemplating a career in theology, you can earn a commission as a Navy Chaplain. Students in accredited theological schools can attend the basic course at the Navy Chaplains School during academic vacations, with full pay and allowances. When they graduate, they become Navy Chaplains.

Not everyone can afford college these days. If you are really interested in becoming an officer in the Navy, you should know about two commissioning programs designed for enlisted men and women of the Navy. One is the Limited Duty Officer Program, which permits career enlisted Navy people to advance to officer status without a college education. Enlisted men and women interested in this program should start planning for it early in their career. The other is the Enlisted Commissioning Program, which enables outstanding enlisted men and women who have already accumulated some college credit to complete the requirements for the bachelor's degree and then earn a commission by attending Officer Candidate School. Most enlisted men and women can earn the college credit necessary to enter the program while they are serving in the Navy (see Chapter IV).

A word of caution may be advisable here: Not all Navy commissions are equal. Graduates of Officer Candidate Schools and other special programs, such as the enlisted Limited Duty Officer Program, probably can expect only a relatively restricted career as an officer in the Navy. On the other hand, the opportunity to gain officer status does provide an incentive for many enlisted men and women who would not otherwise be able to qualify.

And once you have put on the Navy Blue and Gold, there may be no stopping you.

Chapter **VII**

The United States Marine Corps

The United States Marine Corps may be thought of as the Navy's "army," though that has not always been the case. With only about 200,000 members, the Marine Corps is one of the elite fighting forces of the world. The Corps, as it is often called, is a proud force, predominantly male, and young: about three fourths of all Marine enlisted personnel are between the ages of seventeen and twenty-five. And, although Marine infantrymen are routinely—and affectionately—called "grunts," more than ninety-five percent of new Marine Corps recruits are high school graduates, and the Corps' goal is to make that one hundred percent.

The Marine Corps operates under the Secretary of the Navy but is in many respects organized as a separate military service. Indeed, it is one of the "senior services." Along with the Army and the Navy, the United States Marine Corps was established by the Continental Congress in 1775, many months before the Declaration of Independence.

Marines all over the world still celebrate the founding of the Corps each year on November 10 with much pomp and ceremony and great good cheer. And the phrase "Marines around the world" is no exaggeration, because every American Embassy and Consulate abroad is guarded by a Marine Corps contingent. In many of these installations, the annual celebration has become a social highlight of the season, attended by foreign dignitaries and members of the diplomatic corps. The full-dress ball that marks the occasion is usually kicked off with a stirring rendition of the "Marine Hymn." Join in the ceremony, and you'll be singing the familiar words: "From the Halls of Montezuma to the shores of Tripoli ... "

The last three words recall a famous venture in the early 1800s that seems to sum up two Marine Corps slogans: "First to fight," and "Semper Fidelis"—always faithful, the Corps' motto. That bit of Marine Corps history helps to illustrate the changes over the more than two centuries of the Corps' existence as its image changed from one of small security detachments of "leathernecks" crowded aboard the capital ships of the Navy to one of a highly trained, thoroughly modern, and versatile combined-arms ground force with its own air support capable of operating anywhere in the world.

At the turn of the nineteenth century the Pasha of Tripoli, a small country along the North African shore of the Mediterranean Sea that is now known as Libya, decided that the transit fees he had been extracting from American merchant ships sailing off his shores were not sufficient to support his life-style. He therefore had the flagstaff outside the American Consulate cut down. Then, just in case the Americans didn't get the message, he declared war on the United States—the first declaration of war on the young nation by a foreign power.

The American government reponded by sending several Navy ships to the Mediterranean, but not everything was easy. The Pasha of Tripoli soon captured one of the ships, refitted it, and used it to reinforce his demands on American and other merchant ships. You may recall that Stephen Decatur, a young Navy lieutenant, became a national hero as a result of his daring recapture of the ship, the frigate *Philadelphia*, in February 1804.

Later in the same year a handful of Marines serving aboard the USS *Argus* under the command of Lt. Presley Neville O'Bannon were assigned a special mission: to form and train an armed unit and capture the fortified town of Derna, a stronghold of the so-called Barbary pirates. Moving to a base near Alexandria, Egypt, O'Bannon and his seven Marines assembled a ragtag force of about 500 Arabs, Greeks, and Turks. Early in 1805, O'Bannon's little army marched 600 miles across the Libyan desert and, with the assistance of a bombardment from three U.S. Navy ships just offshore, seized the fort. About a month later, on June 4, 1805, the Pasha signed a peace treaty with the United States. Lieutenant O'Bannon returned home as the "hero of Derna."

Lieutenant O'Bannon's victory at Derna was neither the first nor the last of the legendary exploits celebrated by today's Marine Corps. The battle streamers on the flag at Marine Corps headquarters honor scores of combat actions around the world, from the Revolutionary War to Grenada. The Marine Corps emblem itself symbolizes a tradition of service and valor around the world under exceptional conditions: An eagle is perched on a globe, which is in turn superimposed on an anchor. The eagle represents the United States. The globe symbolizes worldwide service. The anchor recalls the origin of the Corps as a naval organization.

Most of the men and women of the Marine Corps are stationed "ashore," these days. Only about 5,000 of its 200,000 members are "afloat." Some of these Marines still serve in the traditional security detachments aboard ships of the U.S. Navy. Others belong to the amphibious units assigned to Navy units operating at sea. But by far the largest number of men and women Marines serve in the Fleet Marine Force (FMF), the elite fighting arm of the Corps.

MISSION AND ORGANIZATION OF THE MARINE CORPS

Within the Department of Defense, the Marine Corps has responsibility for developing the doctrine, tactics, techniques, and equipment employed by landing forces in amphibious operations. Though the Marine Corps is part of the United States Navy and under the authority of the Secretary of the Navy, in practice the Corps often operates as a separate military service in military training and combat operations. On the other hand, the Corps depends on the Navy for various support activities.

For example, the Navy provides transportation to Marine Corps units, which are trained primarily to land on beaches in foreign or enemy territory. The Navy also provides artillery fire and much of the air support to Marine Corps units engaged in over-the-beach operations until they can land their own armored vehicles and artillery and develop ground facilities for their own tactical and utility aircraft. Marine Corps aviation units may operate from Navy aircraft carriers during the initial phase of an operation. Moreover, the Navy provides personnel to man the beach parties that initially control the beachhead and the naval gunfire detachments that coordinate artillery support.

Navy support to the Marines continues even after the beachhead has been established. For example, the Navy provides medical personnel and services, chaplains, and supplies and equipment to the Marine units on the beach.

The close relationship between the Marine Corps and the Navy has other aspects, too. The Marine security detachments aboard ships of the Navy are part of the ship's complement and under the control of the ship's captain. A battalion of Marines is usually afloat aboard Navy troopships with the Sixth Fleet in the Mediterranean Sea. Up to a regiment of Marines can be sealifted to "hot spots" by the Seventh Fleet, operating in the Pacific. Other Marine detachments provide security services to U.S. Navy shore installations, in the United States and abroad.

Marine Corps Headquarters

The headquarters of the United States Marine Corps is in Washington, D.C., and consists of the Commandant of the Marine

Corps and the staff agencies that assist him in performing his functions and responsibilities.

The Commandant of the Corps is directly responsible to the Secretary of the Navy for all activities of the Marine Corps. His responsibilities include determining the characteristics of equipment and materiel to be developed and purchased for the Corps and prescribing the training required to prepare Marines for combat duty. The Commandant also provides technical advice to the Secretary of the Navy and his civilian assistants and to the Chief of Naval Operations regarding policies and procedures for Navy establishments ashore. The Commandant may also exercise command authority over some of the Navy's shore establishment.

In general terms, then, the Commandant of the Marine Corps is co-equal to the Chief of Naval Operations. To illustrate this point, it may be pointed out that he is a full member of the Joint Chiefs of Staff, the coordinating body of the Department of Defense.

Marine Corps Major Commands

Most of the Marine Corps major commands are oriented toward combat operations. As a result of Congressional action, the main forces of the Corps are the three Marine Divisions and the three Marine Air Wings that make up the Fleet Marine Force. Each Marine Division trains and operates in close coordination with one of the Marine Air Wings to form an air-ground team. The air-ground team is provided various support units to make up a self-sufficient Marine Amphibious Force. With these general principles in mind, it is fairly easy to name the Corps' major combat or tactical commands:

Fleet Marine Force, Atlantic	Norfolk, Virginia
Fleet Marine Force, Pacific	Camp Smith, Hawaii
First Marine Amphibious Force	Camp Pendleton, California
Second Marine Amphibious Force	Camp Lejeune, North Carolina
Third Marine Amphibious Force	Camp Butler, Okinawa

Note that the three Marine Amphibious Forces are not generally afloat on ships of the U.S. Navy, though one or more combat-ready composite Marine battalions, together with their attached Marine air units, may be seaborne at any time. The units at sea with the fleet are rotated through short tours of duty as part of the Marine Corps training program.

The Marine Corps also includes two other major commands, in addition to the tactical commands:

Marine Corps Development and Education Command	Quantico, Virginia
Marine Corps Air-Ground Combat Center	Twenty Nine Palms, California

The first of these commands satisfies the requirement that the Commandant of the Marine Corps develop the doctrine, the tactics, and the training of Marines required for combat and other roles. In conformity with the worldwide mission of the Marine Corps, it includes a section for winter and mountain operations, among others. That is to say, the Corps no longer limits itself to training for amphibious assaults.

The Air-Ground Center develops and tests doctrine and tactics for Marine Corps operations and provides facilities for air-ground training.

Unlike the other primary military services, the Marine Corps does not have major commands that coordinate or carry out such functions as medical services, logistical services, and intelligence and security. As a general rule, such services are provided by the Navy; Marine Corps personnel may be assigned to such Navy service commands and units. The absence of these major commands in the Marine Corps structure is what makes the Corps "lean and mean": Preparation for combat is its principal concern.

The Corps' "total force" approach also includes the Fourth Marine Amphibious Force, a Marine Corps Reserve organization that has headquarters in New Orleans, Louisiana. The Fourth Marine Amphibious Force has the same structure as the active amphibious forces; assigned Marine Corps Reserve units regularly train with active Marine Corps units, including participation in field exercises and maneuvers in the United States and abroad.

ENLISTING IN THE MARINE CORPS

The United States Marine Corps is the smallest of the four regular military services; it has only 200,000 members. Each year the Corps recruits about 50,000 young men and women to maintain its ranks. Recruiting goals have been exceeded in each of the recent years for which data are available.

The Corps' recruiting slogan says a good deal: "We're looking for a few good men." But it could say something else, such as, "We're looking for a few good young men and women who have high school diplomas.'' For the enlisted personnel of the Marine Corps as a group are younger than those of any other regular military service; and new Marine recruits are better educated than those of any service except the United States Air Force: about ninety-five percent have completed high school. The Corps has announced that its goal is for all enlisted men and women to have a high school diploma or equivalent. Special inducements are now aimed at prospective recruits who have some post–high school education.

On the other hand, only about five percent (one in twenty) of all Marines are women. This does not mean that the Marine Corps is trying to keep women away, however. Women have served in the Corps for seventy years. And, in fact, qualified females are encouraged to apply for training as Marines and eventual assignment to all Marine Corps jobs except for some combat, combat support, and aviation specialties.

Though the procedure for enlistment in the Marine Corps is not much different than that for the other military services, the physical and mental requirements may be somewhat tougher to meet. Recruiters also look for evidence of individual motivation, self-discipline, and ability to work as a member of a team.

Applicants for the Marine Corps must be citizens or permanent

PHOTO BY CHUCK DEMAR

A woman marine tests equipment as part of her job in the weather caster field.

residents who are between the ages of seventeen and twenty-nine and in excellent health. Graduation from high school is not yet a requirement, though a high school diploma is highly desirable. The Marine Corps will arrange for otherwise qualified applicants to delay entry on active duty while they are completing high school or post-secondary schooling.

Marine Corps enlistments may be for three, four, five, or six years of active duty; the balance of a total of eight years must be served in a Marine Corps Reserve status unless the Marine reenlists.

Qualified applicants can be guaranteed training in both ground and aviation specialties under a wide variety of enlistment options. Scores on the Armed Services Vocational Aptitude Battery influence the applicant's eligibility for any Marine Corps specialty.

Male high school graduates who enlist in the Marine Corps may qualify for bonuses of up to five thousand dollars by enlisting for four to six years and selecting training in a combat arms specialty or one of several other specialties including radar repairman, aircraft weapons specialist, aviation radio repairman, and air traffic controller.

Enlistment Options with Accelerated Promotion

The Marine Corps offers several enlistment options that provide for accelerated promotion. They include the Quality Enlistment Program, the College Enlistment Program, and the Musician Enlistment Option.

The Quality Enlistment Program is designed for highly qualified high school graduates who enlist for six years. Successful applicants can select their occupational field and a geographical area for their initial assignment. Those who enlist for combat arms or other specific specialties (see above) may qualify for handsome enlistment bonuses. Accelerated promotions up to the grade of E-4 (Corporal) are part of the program.

The College Enlistment Program is intended for applicants age eighteen and older who have either completed requirements for an associate degree at a community college or have accumulated sixty semester hours (ninety quarter hours) from an accredited institution; holders of certificates from certain postsecondary vocational school courses may also be eligible. Those who are particularly well qualified may be able to enlist under the delayed-entry program and continue their studies for six months to a year.

Applicants who qualify under the College Enlistment Program can hand-pick their occupational specialty. They are appointed to pay grade E-2 (Private First Class) and paid at that grade during recruit training. However, the Private First Class stripes are not issued until the recruit graduates from boot camp. Promotion to Lance Corporal (E-3) occurs six months after reporting for active duty. Promotion to Corporal (E-4) normally follows seven months later.

The Musician Enlistment Option is available only to qualified musicians; an audition is required. Successful applicants attend the Marine Corps School of Music for about six months after they complete recruit training. Upon completion of the Music School course, they are assigned to Marine Corps field bands or to drum and bugle units. The program offers accelerated promotions and opportunities for advanced music training. The current director of the Marine Corps Band, a Marine Colonel, was a participant in a similar enlistment program many years ago.

Training to Become a Marine

Once you have gotten past the initial interviews and qualification tests and actually enlisted in the Marine Corps, you are sent to a Marine Corps basic training program. Boot camp, as it is called, is a grueling, demanding course of instruction and physical conditioning designed to transform young civilians into disciplined members of the United States Marine Corps. It is conducted at Parris Island, South Carolina, and San Diego, California. Women Marines take basic training only at Parris Island.

The basic training given new Marine Corps enlistees is similar to that given by other military services, but it has traditionally been much more rigorous, with greater demands on both physical and mental abilities.

A Marine Corps recruiting pamphlet says frankly, "Boot camp is no picnic. Most Marines say they'd never go through it again. But you'll never hear Marines say they're sorry they did it."

The objective of boot camp is to instill confidence in the recruits, to teach them to work well in groups, and to generate pride in being a member of the Marine Corps. At the end of the training you will know what "Semper Fidelis" really means. The motto, abbreviated to "Semper Fi," becomes something of a private password between Marines. The system works, but not every new recruit can make the grade. If you don't make the grade, you are discharged from the Corps.

Some male recruits who fail the initial physical fitness tests are given a second chance, however. They are taken out of their recruit training class and assigned to a Physical Conditioning Platoon. There they receive physical and psychological conditioning over several weeks so that they can resume full-scale recruit training. About one third of those assigned to a Physical Conditioning Platoon are eventually discharged from the Corps.

One consolation for new recruits may be that every one of the drill instructors at boot camp had to do it all over again in preparation for assignment as an instructor. Another compensation for those recruits who excel is that they may be promoted to Private First Class upon graduation.

While at boot camp, each Marine recruit undergoes a review of personal qualifications and receives a final job classification. Recruits are then earmarked for technical school training or for an immediate job assignment. About 75 to 80 percent of boot camp graduates go directly to formal schools for specialty training following a brief leave. Some of these schools are operated by the Marine Corps; some by other military services. Marines who do not attend a formal school receive on-the-job training in their first assignment.

MARINE CORPS ENLISTED OCCUPATIONS

Every Marine is trained to perform a specific job, often a job that could mean life or death to someone else. More than 300 jobs in three

PHOTO BY CHUCK DEMAR

A United States Marine prepares to test a marine jet engine in his sound-proof booth.

dozen career fields are available to enlistees after basic training. More than 400 Marine Corps jobs exist, but some are available only as you advance in experience and training. Training in specific career fields may be requested prior to enlistment by those who enter the Quality Enlistment Program. Men and women who qualify for the College Enlistment Program may select specific jobs. The table below shows Marine Corps occupational fields and numerical codes. The right-hand column lists the Military Occupations included in each occupational field. The table is not official and is not necessarily complete. Consult your recruiter to be sure your special job interest is included in any career field that may appeal to you.

Note that there are no medical, dental, or other health-related specializations in the Marine Corps. Marines use Navy medical facilities when available; as needed, the Navy details medical specialists to Marine Corps units to provide medical services.

Training in special fields not shown in the table is available to Marines who are already on active duty and have the appropriate qualifications. Among them are:

Career Information and Counseling (Caseworker/Counselor)
Chapel Management Specialist (Religious Program Specialist)
Drill Instructor (Trainer)
Marine Security Guard (Embassy duty; not in Appendix C)
Recruiter (Recruiting Specialist)

Marines are usually assigned to these duties on a voluntary basis for one tour of duty outside their normal career field.

ENLISTED CAREER DEVELOPMENT

Graduation from boot camp launches the Marine recruit into the mainstream of the Corps. Each occupational field has well-defined career development guidelines. Once you have completed your specialty training and are assigned to a Marine Corps job, you are coached by a career counselor who is a specially trained senior noncommissioned officer. The role of the career counselor is to help individual Marines to make the most of their experience and service while they are in the Corps.

Each Marine Corps specialty is designed to provide increasingly challenging and varied assignments, advanced training in the specialty as well as in leadership and management skills, and opportunities to exercise supervisory responsibilities. A number of Marine Corps specialties are included under the apprenticeship program

MARINE CORPS ENLISTED OCCUPATIONS

Marine Corps Designation (and Field Code)	Military Occupation (See Appendix C)
Air Control/Air Support/Anti-Air Warfare (Occupational Field 72)	Radar and Sonar Operator; Artillery Crew Member; Radio Operator, Aircraft Launch and Recovery Specialist
Aircraft Maintenance (60/61)	Aircraft Mechanic, Aircraft Electrician, Survival Equipment Specialist, Maintenance Data Analyst
Airfield Services (70)	Flight Operations Specialist, Firefighter
Air Traffic Control and Enlisted Flight Crews (73)	Air Crew Member, Air Traffic Controller, Radio Operator, Aircraft Launch and Recovery Specialist
Ammunition and Explosive Ordnance Disposal (23)	Ordnance Mechanic, Stock and Inventory Specialist, Shipping and Supply Specialist
Auditing, Finance, and Accounting (34)	Accounting Specialist
Aviation Ordance (65)	Ordnance Mechanic
Avionics (63/64)	Aircraft Electrician, Electronic Instrument Repairer, Electronic Weapons System Repairer, Precision Instrument Repairer
Band (55)	Musicians
Data/Communications Maintenance (28)	Electronic Instrument Repairer, Electronic Weapons System Repairer, Radio Repairer, Teletype Repairer, Telephone Repairer, Precision Instrument Repairer, Radar and Sonar Repairer
Data Systems (40)	Data Entry Specialist, Computer Operator, Computer Programmer, Computer Systems Analyst
Drafting, Surveying, Mapping (14)	Drafter, Mapping Technician, Surveying Technician
Electronics Maintenance (59)	Radio Repairer, Precision Instrument Repairer, Electronic Weapons System Repairer, Radar/Sonar Repairer, Telephone Repairer, Teletype Repairer, Data Processing Equipment Repairer, Electronic Instrument Repairer
Engineer, Construction and Equipment (13)	Combat Engineer, Construction Equipment Operator, Fuel and Chemical Lab Technician, Iron Worker, Heavy Equipment Mechanic, Paving Equipment Operator, Sheet Metal Worker
Field Artillery (08)	Artillery Crew Member, Radar and Sonar Operator, Weather Observer
Food Services (33)	Food Service Specialist
Infantry (03)	Infantryman

Intelligence (02)	Intelligence Specialist
Legal Services (44)	Legal Technician, Court Reporter
Logistics (04)	Flight Operations Specialist, Survival Equipment Specialist, Stock And Inventory Specialist
Marine Corps Exchange (41)	Food Service Specialist, Sales and Stock Specialist
Military Police and Corrections (58)	Correction Specialist, Detective, Military Police
Motor Transport (35)	Automobile Mechanic, Automobile Body Specialist, Dispatcher, Truck Driver
Nuclear, Biological, Chemical (57)	Emergency Management Specialist
Operational Communications (25)	Radio Operator, Telephone Line Installer/Repairer, Telephone Operator, Teletype Operator, Radio Repairer, Teletype Repairer
Ordnance (21)	Heavy Equipment Mechanic, Ordnance Mechanic, Machinist, Precision Instrument Repairer
Personnel and Administration (01)	Administrative Support Specialist, Personnel Specialist, Secretary/ Stenographer, Postal Specialist
Printing and Reproduction (15)	Printing Specialist
Public Affairs (43)	Reporter/Newswriter, Radio and TV Announcer
Signals Intelligence & Ground Electronic Warfare (26)	Intelligence Specialist, Radio Intelligence Operator, Interpreter and Translator
Supply Administration and Operations (30)	Shipping and Receiving Specialist, Stock and Inventory Specialist
Tank and Amphibian Tractor (18)	Tank Crew Member
Training and Audio Visual Support (46)	Graphic Designer and Illustrator, Broadcast and Recording Technician, Motion Picture Camera Operator, Photographer, Photoprocessing Specialist
Transportation (31)	Transportation Specialist
Utilities (11)	Clothing and Fabric Repairer, Electrician, Electrical Product Repairer, Heating and Cooling Mechanic, Office Machine Repairer, Plumber and Pipefitter
Weather Service (68)	Weather Observer

Note: A number of the above occupational fields include job specialties covered under the Department of Labor's apprentice program. Appendix C will help you identify the specific fields, but you should consult a recruiter to be certain that the apprenticeship program you want is available and in which Marine Corps Occupational Field it is included.

administered by the Department of Labor; you will find them in Appendix C. Successful completion of any apprenticeship program satisfies the requirements for journeyman status in that technical field, an accomplishment that can be of considerable value to a Marine who decides to leave the service and seek employment in the civilian job market.

Promotion in the Marine Corps, as in the other military services, depends to a large extent on the individual's proficiency in a chosen technical field. In addition to courses offered at about 500 technical schools and subsequent on-the-job training, further technical training is available from the Marine Corps Institute, by means of correspondence courses. Lessons and course materials are free.

The Marine Corps is also concerned about development of the whole individual and encourages Marines to improve their general educational level. The Corps offers various incentives, including tuition assistance for off-duty college studies that covers seventy-five percent of tuition charges—up to 90 percent for career Marines at the grade of Sergeant (E-5) and above. Marines can also receive college credit for military and technical school training and experience.

Other Marine Corps programs permit highly qualified enlisted members to complete college while on active duty; some may become Marine Corps officers under these programs. Commissioning programs permit active-duty enlisted members to compete for attendance at the Naval Academy and for a Naval ROTC scholarship and to apply for an officer training program (after attending college for up to eighteen months with full pay and allowances).

Advancement in the Marine Corps

Promotion in the Corps depends both on performance in the individual's military occupational specialty (MOS) and his or her development as a Marine. Promotion becomes increasingly competitive as a Marine advances in rank, since each Marine competes with all other Marines with the same rank and MOS.

Commanding officers are authorized to promote Marines through the rank of Lance Corporal (E-3). Normal time-in-grade requirements below this level are six months from Private (E-1) to Private First Class (E-2), and eight months from Private First Class to Lance Corporal (E-3). As already noted, however, some enlistment programs offer opportunities for accelerated promotion, up to Corporal (E-4). In addition, up to ten percent of the Marine privates who excel during boot camp may be promoted to Private First Class upon graduation.

Promotion into the non-commissioned officer ranks (Corporal, E-4, and Sergeant, E-5) is competitive in most cases, however, and depends upon the needs of the Corps. The normal time in grade for promotion from Lance Corporal to Corporal (E-4) is eight months; for promotion to Sergeant (E-5), twelve months as a Corporal. Promotions into the Staff Non-Commissioned Officer ranks, or E-6 to E-9, are determined by Staff NCO promotion boards that meet each year at Marine Corps Headquarters.

A Career Model for Enlisted Marines

Each Marine Corps specialty has its own career guidelines, but it is possible to sketch a generalized pattern for a Marine Corps career that may extend over twenty to thirty years. The career pattern is divided into five phases: Recruit Training, Initial Career Development, Intermediate Career Development, Advanced Career Development, and Senior Supervisor. Since you have already completed recruit training, let us see what is in store for you. We shall start with Phase II, because Recruit Training is Phase I.

Phase II, Initial Career Development. Three to four years are anticipated in this phase, which includes introductory technical training and development of leadership skills. Assignment during this phase is usually to the Fleet Marine Force (a Marine Division or an Air Wing, depending upon your specialty). By the end of the period, you should have been promoted to Corporal, at least, and possibly to Sergeant. If you enlisted for four years or less, reenlistment at the end of this phase offers you the opportunity for a new assignment and advanced training; otherwise you are transferred to the Marine Corps Reserve.

Phase III, Intermediate Career Development. During the next five to six years you have opportunities for advanced schooling in your MOS as well as some leadership training; your supervisory responsibilities increase. During this period, you advance into the Staff NCO ranks. Assignments outside the Fleet Marine Force are available, including special duty assignments: Sea Duty, Barracks Duty, Embassy Security Guard, Drill Instructor, Reserve Unit Inspector and Instructor, or Recruiter, for example.

Phase IV, Advanced Career Development. During the next five to six years, with a great deal of experience already behind you, the emphasis is on development of leadership abilities. You may attend the Advanced NCO Academy or receive management training, or both. You should make Gunnery Sergeant (E-7) during this phase and be eligible for staff assignments and/or assignment to some independent operation or activity, as NCO-in-Charge. Duty as a Service School Instructor is likely.

Phase V, Senior Supervisor. With thirteen to sixteen years' service as a Marine, you are now at the peak of your career. You can anticipate assignments with important leadership, management, and policy-making responsibilities: Senior Instructor, Technical Department Head, Headquarters Staff assignments, or NCOIC of a separate Marine Corps detachment. Your responsibilities increase as you rise through the ranks from Gunnery Sergeant to First Sergeant or Master Sergeant (E-8) and finally cap your career as a Sergeant Major or Master Gunnery Sergeant (E-9)—perhaps even Sergeant Major of the Marine Corps.

Marines in the Staff Non-Commissioned Officer ranks command a great deal of respect for their broad experience, leadership qualities, and educational accomplishments. Climbing the career ladder is not easy; fewer than ten percent of all Marine enlisted men and women get to serve in the first three NCO grades (E-7 to E-9). The Marine Corps provides the opportunity for a great career, but only you can make that opportunity work for you by taking advantage of the technical training, leadership and management training, and educational programs available. Along the way, remember that the recruiting posters do not say that the Marine Corps guarantees you anything. What they do say is: "We're looking for a few GOOD men."

BECOMING A MARINE CORPS OFFICER

The routes to a commission in the Marine Corps are similar to those of the other military services, but the emphasis on the Officer Candidate School as a primary source of officers is unique. Statistics show that about nine out of ten newly commissioned Marine Corps officers earned their bars by successful completion of an Officer Candidate School program.

A college degree is a prerequisite for a Marine Corps commission; attendance at Officer Candidate School is generally restricted to those who are in a degree program or already have a degree. All the commissioning programs are, however, open to active and reserve Marine Corps enlisted men and women as well as to civilians. One might conclude that another Marine Corps slogan is, "Marines are made, not born."

Marine Corps commissions can also be earned by attendance at the Naval Academy and through participation in a Naval ROTC program at selected colleges and universities—though even NROTC graduates are required to attend Officer Candidate School. Few, if any, direct commissions are granted by the Marine Corps.

All Marine Corps commissioned officers, including prospective aviators, are trained to be combat arms leaders, though they may specialize later. The only professionals actively recruited by the Marine Corps are lawyers, and even they are trained initially as combat leaders. The Marine Corps has no medical personnel or chaplains; the functions are performed by Navy officers.

On the other hand, the Marine Corps commissioning programs are a source of young officers with varied college backgrounds, some of which are of immediate value to the Corps. A Marine Second Lieutenant may, for example, be a graduate civil engineer. An early assignment might be to a combat engineer unit; his specialty training is at the Engineer Indoctrination School at Camp Lejeune. Later in his career he may be sent to the Naval Post Graduate School or to a civilian university for graduate studies in an engineering field of special interest to the Corps. Meanwhile, he will have moved upward through the officer ranks with progressively responsible command and staff assignments in the Fleet Marine Force, as an instructor at the Engineer School or with a Marine Corps Reserve unit, and, eventually, to a senior staff position in a joint command or at Headquarters, U.S. Marine Corps. The leadership training and field experience gained during early assignments in the Fleet Marine Force are an essential part of his development as a Marine officer.

Not all Marine officers are assigned to the Fleet Marine Force, of course. Aside from the ground combat arms and combat support specialties, the Marine Corps needs officers in the fields of aviation, communications, data processing, supply, law, public relations, and many other specialties. Opportunities exist for female officers in all fields except those prohibited by law, namely, combat arms and combat support specialties and certain Marine Corps aviation specialties.

Commissioning Programs

Those interested in becoming Marine Corps officers can choose from several fairly similar routes to a commission. One important difference between these approaches is the kind of commission earned: that is, a Regular or a Reserve commission.

If you are interested in a career as a Regular Marine officer but do not have a great deal of money for college costs, you should consider competing either for appointment to the Naval Academy or for a four-year Marine-option Naval ROTC scholarship. Several hundred

NROTC scholarships are available each year to high school seniors and enrolled college students.

Both programs are open to high school students and to Marines on active duty who are high school graduates. Both programs pay the costs of tuition, fees, textbooks, and uniforms. Appointment to the Naval Academy also includes full board and room and an allowance of several hundred dollars a month. A Naval ROTC scholarship includes an allowance of one hundred dollars a month but does not cover board and room. On the other hand, the ROTC scholarship program requires the student to participate in sixteen weeks of intensive military training spread over three summers; participants are paid at the pay grade of E-5 during this training. The pay for summer training can help to meet the costs of board and room during the subsequent school year. Regular Marine Corps commissions are awarded to graduates of both programs. See Chapter IV for additional details.

The vast majority of Marine Corps officers earn Reserve commissions while attending the college or university of their choice. One way to do this is to elect the "Marine option" of the regular four-year Naval ROTC program (See Appendix D). You pay your own way, for the most part, and you have to work just as hard as the scholarship students, but when you graduate you pin on the same gold Lieutenant's bars.

The most popular route to a Marine Corps commission for men is probably the Platoon Leaders' Class (PLC), which can start as early as the end of the freshman year of college and as late as the junior year. A commissioning program for male college seniors or recent graduates requires that they attend a ten-week Officer Candidate Class (OCC). Female students can earn Marine Corps commissions through the Women Officer Candidate Program (WOCP), available to qualified applicants following the junior year in college or after graduation. Attendance at a ten-week Officer Candidate School designed for females is required.

During actual training, the Marine Corps pays candidates at the grade of E-5 (Sergeant); travel expenses, books, and uniforms are also provided. Depending upon the academic year in which any of these programs is started, financial assistance amounting to one hundred dollars a month during the school year may be available. That is, a male student who completes PLC training at the end of his freshman year may apply for financial assistance for each of the next three years; one who took PLC training at the end of his junior year could expect financial assistance only during the senior year.

Successful candidates receive a Reserve commission when they graduate from college or, if already graduated, upon completion of OCS. Acceptance of the commission obligates the new Marine officer to serve on active duty for at least three years; longer if the candidate accepted financial assistance.

All the commissioning programs described above except the Women Officer Candidate Program offer both ground and aviation officer options. Election of the aviation option may afford ROTC and PLC undergraduate candidates an opportunity to complete preflight training. Actual flight training is deferred until after completion of the Marine Corps Basic School. Completion of flight training obligates Marine officers to serve on active duty for four or five years after certification.

A Law Option is available to participants in the PLC, OCC, and WOCP programs. Under this program, candidates are commissioned upon graduation from college but not required to perform active duty until completion of law school and admission to the bar. Participants in this program are responsible for their own educational expenses; some officers may be able to participate in Marine Corps Reserve training and earn extra income while attending law school.

Several commissioning programs are specifically designed for active-duty Marine enlisted men and women. In general, they make it possible to complete requirements for a college degree and then attend Officer Candidate School. These programs are normally available only to seasoned Marines, however, not to enlistees.

The Marine Corps, like the Army and the Navy, has a group of specialists called Warrant Officers—about 1,500, in fact. They perform many middle-level management functions and are appointed directly from the ranks of active-duty Marine enlisted men and women, usually those at the Staff NCO level.

Officer Career Development

Officer career development in the Marine Corps begins with Officer Candidate School, at Quantico, Virginia. Marine Corps OCS is a "boot camp" for would-be officers; it is here that you find out whether you are suited to be a Marine officer. Only the best-qualified candidates earn commissions.

Following commissioning and entry on active duty, Marine Corps officers attend a twenty-one-week Basic Officer School. The course material is designed to equip them with the professional knowledge needed to command and lead Marines. During Basic School, officers are evaluated and specialty training is assigned. The new officers participate in this process, and a reported ninety percent of them are assigned in the specialty area of their choice. In some cases, however, the needs of the service come first.

Officers who have elected an aviation option attend Basic School along with other newly commissioned officers. Those who elect the law option attend Basic School after they have been admitted to the bar.

Specialty training follows the completion of Basic School. Officers may be assigned to a formal school or directly to a duty station for on-the-job training. Those who have elected an aviation option are assigned to flight training.

The chart shows how officers are assigned within the various occupational fields in the Corps. About half of all Marine officers begin their careers in fields related to aviation.

Approximately another third enter service in the combat arms and combat support elements of the Corps. The remainder are assigned to a wide variety of jobs related to administration, communications, supply and maintenance, public affairs, intelligence and security, legal affairs, and other support for the Corps' operational forces.

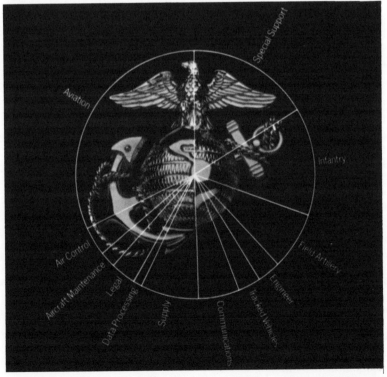

U.S. MARINE CORPS PHOTO

Marine officer careers are not limited by the field of initial assignment. As they gain experience, in fact, Marine Corps officers are expected to be able to do about anything. Along the way are out-of-specialty opportunities to serve as instructors in service schools or with Marine Corps Reserve units, as commanders of Marine honor guard units, as military attachés at American embassies abroad, and even as White House aides. The present Commandant of the Marine Corps once commanded the Fourth Marine Division, a Reserve unit.

Moreover, the Marine Corps offers many opportunities for officers to improve their educational horizons and qualifications by attending postgraduate programs at the Naval Post Graduate School, at the Air Force Institute of Technology, or at a civilian university.

The content of the Marine Basic School course is intended to serve officers in the company grades (Second Lieutenant to Captain), or during the first eight to ten years of commissioned service. Most Reserve officers fulfill their service obligation before the end of this time. Consequently, most officers in the grade of Major and above hold Regular commissions. However, the Marine Corps does have a procedure that permits highly qualified Reserve officers to convert their status to that of Regular officers. Moreover, many Reserve officers are able to remain on active duty for extended periods, though they serve without any career guarantees.

Beyond Basic School are such advanced Marine Corps institutions as the Command and Staff College (for Captains and Majors), the Marine Corps Service Support Schools, and the Marine Corps Engineer School. Marine Corps officers may also be sent to schools operated by other services, depending upon their specialization, and to joint-service schools such as the Defense Language School or the Defense Public Affairs School.

Training for Marine officers (Majors/Lieutenant Colonels) who may serve with joint and combined military commands is conducted by the Armed Forces Staff College, Norfolk, Virgina. Serior Marine Corps officers (Lt. Colonel/Colonel) may be selected to attend senior national military colleges where the emphasis is on strategy: the National War College (politicomilitary affairs) or the Industrial College of the Armed Forces (economic and industrial matters related to national security and national mobilization).

Like the Marine Corps itself, the body of career Marine officers is a small but elite group—fewer than nine thousand, perhaps. But whether you aspire to a career in the Marine Corps or would be content just to serve a tour of several years, service as a Marine Corps officer offers you a challenging, varied experience that can rarely be equaled in the military services.

Chapter VIII

The United States Coast Guard

The smallest of the military services of the United States, with only about 39,000 members in the active force and a reserve element of about 12,000, the Coast Guard is probably also the least known. But, though the Coast Guard is small, it has a big mission, and much of that mission is carried out twenty-four hours a day, every day of the year, around a large part of the globe. As one Coast Guard publication puts it: "We don't just practice for things that may happen someday."

The men and women of the Coast Guard are intensely proud of their service and live by its motto: "Semper Paratus"—Always Ready. While the Coast Guard is organized, trained, and equipped as a naval service, it proudly maintains its status of independence from the United States Navy. Coast Guard vessels may resemble Navy ships, but they are known as the "white fleet" and are easily distinguishable by the bright red-orange diagonal stripes painted on their bows. The color of the stripes is that of international marine distress flags and symbolizes, perhaps, the humanitarian role of many Coast Guard missions. Even the uniforms now worn by members of the Coast Guard are distinctive, though they were once identical to those of the Navy except for differences in insignia.

The missions of the Coast Guard frequently require its members to perform under extremely hazardous conditions and often expose them to physical danger. For those reasons, the Coast Guard recruits men and women who are able to "keep their heads" and remain calm and effective in the face of danger. The law-enforcement functions of the Coast Guard also make it essential that its members have that elusive quality known as "integrity."

Incidentally, the name "Coast Guard" is something of a misnomer today. The Coast Guard performs many of its tasks on inland waterways such as the Mississippi River or the Great Lakes. In fact, I was first introduced to the Coast Guard in Cleveland, Ohio, when I had to obtain the necessary papers to qualify me for a job as deckhand on an ore freighter on regular runs from the ore fields at the head of Lake Superior to the steel mills along the shores of Lake Erie.

More recently, on the island of Grenada, in the Caribbean, I met a young Coast Guard officer who was the skipper of a cutter that normally operates in the Great Lakes. On short notice, he and his crew had sailed the cutter out of the Lakes, down the St. Lawrence River to the Atlantic Ocean, and thence south to the Caribbean—no mean navigational feat—on a "show the flag" mission. The season was mid-winter, and the cutter ordinarily would have been laid up at a pier because of the ice in the Great Lakes. The crew was obviously enjoying the sunshine of Grenada, but they were already preparing for the return voyage to the Lakes—in time for the spring thaw.

WHAT THE COAST GUARD DOES

As you might expect, the mission of the Coast Guard is closely interwoven with its history. So let us look briefly at how the modern Coast Guard developed in order to understand better what it does.

The United States Coast Guard has existed in its present form only since 1915, when the Revenue Cutter Service and the Lifesaving Service were merged into one agency.

The Revenue Cutter Service or, as it was originally known, the Revenue Marine, was formed in 1790 at the suggestion of Alexander Hamilton, then Secretary of the Treasury, for the specific purpose of protecting the revenues that the federal government derived from duties and taxes on goods imported from foreign countries. This may not seem such an important matter today, but customs revenues were the single most important source of income for the government until about the time the United States entered World War I, in 1916.

Over the course of a century, therefore, the armed cutters of the Revenue Marine performed a very important function for the Treasury Department. The job of enforcing federal customs laws soon involved the Revenue Marine in a campaign to stop the smuggling of foreign goods into the country. Revenue Marine operations along the coast included boarding and searching foreign vessels suspected of smuggling, and sometimes seizing illegal cargoes and the ships themselves. A risky business, indeed. For a decade or more, the Revenue Marine was, in fact, the only armed naval force maintained by the new government, since the Navy had been disbanded after the Revolutionary War.

During those early years, the functions of the Revenue Marine gradually broadened to include enforcement of federal immigration laws, responsibility for port security, operations against pirates, a concern for marine safety, and responsibility for enforcing general maritime law. Out of that heritage grew the role of the modern Coast Guard in interdicting the flow of narcotics from producing nations into the United States, for example, though the service is now part of the Department of Transportation.

The Lifesaving Service was quite another thing. Established as a governmental agency only in 1878, the Lifesaving Service had grown out of the efforts of such private organizations as the Humane Society of Massachusetts to do something to reduce the great loss of life from shipwrecks along the eastern coast of the United States.

In the early 1800s the Humane Society erected the first shelters for shipwreck survivors along the south coast of Massachusetts Bay, at Cohasset. The Society also supplied lifeboats to aid in rescue attempts; the lifeboats were manned by volunteers. By the middle of the century, the federal government had organized lifesaving stations along the coast of New Jersey and on Long Island.

The establishment of the Lifesaving Service itself is credited to Sumner Kimball, a native of Maine, whose studies of shipwrecks along the coast led him to recommend the organization of a more responsible government lifesaving program. At the time Kimball was in charge of the Revenue Marine. He left that post to head the new Lifesaving Service and remained in that position until the service was merged with the Revenue Cutter Service in 1915.

Before that year, however, the Revenue Cutter Service had already been charged with conducting the international ice patrol following the loss of the *Titanic* in a collision with an iceberg in the North Atlantic in 1912.

Still later, in 1939, the independent Lighthouse Service was absorbed by the Coast Guard. The responsibilities of the former Bureau of Marine Inspection and Navigation were transferred to the Coast Guard in 1942. In 1971 the Federal Boat Safety Act gave the Coast Guard greatly increased responsibilities in the field of recreational boating, which until that time had largely been reserved to the states.

Thus the original role of the Revenue Marine as an armed naval force deployed against smugglers has been expanded over the past two centuries. The modern Coast Guard remains an armed force organized and trained as a military service and responsible primarily for law enforcement; in time of war or other emergency, the service may operate as a highly specialized arm of the United States Navy. But the modern Coast Guard has meanwhile assumed many other peacetime missions that give its members extraordinary opportunities for a career of service to the nation.

In addition to the continuing mission of enforcing maritime law and helping to enforce the customs and immigration laws of the United States, the Coast Guard now performs these other missions or services:

Search and Rescue, which may range from assistance to recreational boaters in distress to rescue of the crews of sinking or burning merchant ships. During any given year the Coast Guard may respond to 80,000 calls for assistance, save as many as five thousand lives, and render some form of help to another 140,000 persons. Some large Coast Guard cutters are equipped with landing pads for helicopters that assist with the search and rescue operations.

International Ice Patrol. The Coast Guard uses aircraft and cutters to patrol some 45,000 square miles of the North Atlantic Ocean, an area through which passes the heaviest shipping traffic of the entire world. Radar is used to locate and follow icebergs that drift down from the Arctic and pose a threat to marine traffic.

Icebreaking involves the use of cutters and tugs to keep sealanes open in the Arctic and Antarctic regions, in the Great Lakes, and along the Northeast coast of the United States. Two 399-foot cutters recently built for the Coast Guard are capable of continuous forward movement through up to six feet of ice; they can also ram paths through ice as thick as twenty-one feet.

Aids to Navigation provided and maintained by the Coast Guard include more than 48,000 lighthouses, large and small navigational buoys, radio beacons, fog signals, and other devices. A worldwide electronic navigational system for ships and aircraft, LORAN (Long Range Aids to Navigation), is operated and maintained by the Coast Guard. Early in 1986 a Coast Guard LORAN station on a remote Italian island in the Mediterranean Sea was attacked by a Libyan missile patrol boat, presumably in retaliation for the U.S. Navy's raids along the Libyan coast about the same time.

Merchant Marine Safety involves the Coast Guard in every phase of merchant shipping, from approving the design of ships to licensing those who operate them. Coast Guard officers inspect foreign vessels for compliance with safety standards, regulate the loading or unloading of hazardous cargo, and investigate marine accidents. The Coast Guard also prescribes various safety equipment for boats and ships, such as life preservers, firefighting systems, and first-aid equipment, and conducts inspections to ensure compliance with safety regulations. Some of the duties required by the merchant marine safety program are carried out by Coast Guard officers who are stationed abroad, at large seaports in Europe, the Far East, and elsewhere.

Marine Environmental Protection has been a Coast Guard responsibility since 1899, when the first pollution control laws were passed in the United States. Prevention and/or control of oil spills from grounded or damaged oil tankers is one the more familiar tasks of the Coast Guard under this heading. Other concerns involve the transportation of hazardous cargoes, monitoring the activities of foreign fishing fleets off the U.S. coast, and the protection of whales and other marine animals. The Coast Guard has organized several "strike teams" composed of experts in pollution control, marine salvage, diving, and related skills that can be airlifted to sites of marine disasters.

Port Safety activities concern the protection of waterfront facilities and vessels from damage by fire, accident, sabotage, and the like. Coast Guard officers designated Port Captains manage personnel and vessels that are used to patrol harbors, conduct pier and terminal inspections, and investigate marine accidents. Coast Guard personnel operate Automated Vessel Traffic Services in major ports to prevent collisions and groundings in ports and harbors.

Boating Safety responsibilities are carried out under a national boating safety program that affects millions of recreational boaters across the country. In addition to educational programs and close cooperation with state boating authorities, the Coast Guard conducts research on boating safety and boating equipment and enforces boating safety standards. A unique organization of about 40,000 civilian volunteers called the Coast Guard Auxiliary assists with the boating safety program. Members of the Auxiliary organize and conduct courses in seamanship and navigation for the boating public, conduct voluntary safety inspections of privately owned yachts and other marine pleasure craft, and assist in other ways with safety on the water.

ORGANIZATION OF THE COAST GUARD

The Coast Guard is organized along the lines of the United States Navy, but it operates as an independent agency of the Department of Transportation. The Commandant of the Coast Guard is the senior Admiral of the service and is responsible, under the authority of the Secretary of Transportation, for development of policies and procedures for carrying out the missions outlined above, as well as for training and day-to-day operations. The Commandant and his staff also coordinate closely with the Navy and other military services within the Department of Defense on matters related to the wartime mission of the Coast Guard.

The Commandant of the Coast Guard is assisted by a Vice Commandant and by a Chief of Staff who supervises the headquarters staff. The principal staff sections have responsibility for policies and procedures that affect the performance of the various functional missions of the Coast Guard: the Office of Merchant Marine Safety, the Office of Boating Safety, the Office of Marine Environment and Systems, the Office of Engineering, for example. Other headquarters staff sections are concerned with personnel matters, research and development, legal affairs, public affairs, and management of the Coast Guard Reserve.

Operational authority within the Coast Guard is very much decentralized, though there are two major commands: the Atlantic Area command, with headquarters in New York, New York; and the Pacific Area command, in Alameda, California. The Area Commanders coordinate and control major Coast Guard assistance cases within their areas; they may also have specific responsibility for operational readiness and for such activities as polar ice-breaking and operation and maintenance of the automated merchant vessel reporting system. They do not, however, command the twelve Coast Guard Districts located in the United States, Alaska, and Hawaii.

The twelve District Commanders report directly to the Commandant of the Coast Guard on most matters. Each District Commander directs or coordinates the operations of the Coast Guard stations and units and activities within his jurisdiction, including military recruiting. These districts are designated as follows:

1st Coast Guard District	Boston, Massachusetts
2nd Coast Guard Disrict	St. Louis, Missouri
3rd Coast Guard District	Governors Island, New York
5th Coast Guard District	Portsmouth, Virginia
7th Coast Guard District	Miami, Florida
8th Coast Guard District	New Orleans, Louisiana
9th Coast Guard District	Cleveland, Ohio
11th Coast Guard District	Long Beach, California
12th Coast Guard District	San Francisco, California
13th Coast Guard District	Seattle, Washington
14th Coast Guard District	Honolulu, Hawaii
17th Coast Guard District	Juneau, Alaska

The gaps in the sequence of numbers assigned the Districts have occurred largely as a result of the consolidation of two or more former districts.

Some other Coast Guard units and installations are under the

U.S. COAST GUARD PHOTO

One of the functions of the Coast Guard is to patrol our shores against illegal smuggling.

direct control of the Commandant, even though they may be located within the geographical jurisdiction of a District Commander.

The commander of Coast Guard units attached to major DOD commands, or otherwise operating outside the United States, has the status of District Commander and reports directly to the Commandant on Coast Guard matters.

This system results in the delegation of considerable operational authority to Coast Guard officers and senior non-commissioned officers who command operational units and activities that may be located in remote sites. Not long ago, for example, I met a senior Coast Guard petty officer who was responsible for operating and maintaining an important lighthouse on a small island off the coast of Maine. He and his family lived in quarters attached to the lighthouse. No other Coast Guard personnel were stationed on the island. It is for this reason, among others, that the Coast Guard is very careful in its recruiting process.

ENLISTING IN THE COAST GUARD

Enlisting in the Coast Guard is very much like enlisting in any other military service, though the regular enlistment period is four years. The Coast Guard recruits about 5,000 new members from among both male and female high school graduates each year.

Applicants must be at least seventeen years of age and under the age of twenty-six on the day they enlist. They must be in good health and of sound character. All applicants are required to take the Armed Services Vocational Aptitude Battery.

Applicants who meet all the requirements for enlistment may be guaranteed training in their choice of an occupational specialty under the Guaranteed School Program. Qualified applicants may also be able to delay their entry on active duty for up to twelve months if they are high school seniors, or up to six months if they have already graduated from high school.

The Coast Guard has no regular enlistment programs that provide for entry in pay grades above E-1, though opportunities may exist for qualified applicants who have already developed expertise in a skill field needed by the service.

Two dozen occupational career fields are available to enlisted men and women in the Coast Guard. The fields resemble those of the Navy, with some exceptions. They are grouped under four main headings, as shown below. Some equivalent military occupations based on those in Appendix C are listed in the right-hand column, but check with your recruiter to be sure. Most ratings are open to women.

COAST GUARD ENLISTED SPECIALTIES

Coast Guard Rating	*Military Occupation (See Appendix C)*
ADMINISTRATIVE AND SCIENTIFIC SPECIALTIES	
Health Services Technician	Dental Specialist, Medical Service Technician, Radiologic (X-Ray) Technician
Marine Science Technician	Weather Observer
Port Securityman	Firefighter, Detective, Stock and Inventory Specialist
Public Affairs Specialist	Photographer, Reporter and Newswriter, Graphic Designers and Illustrator
Radioman	Computer Operator, Data Entry Specialist, Teletype Operator, Radio Operator
Storekeeper	Accounting Specialist, Shipping and Receiving Specialist, Stock and Inventory Specialist, Sales and Stock Specialist
Subsistence Specialist	Food Service Specialist
Yeoman	Personnel Specialist, Secretary and Stenographer, Court Reporter, Legal Technician, Data Entry Specialist
AVIATION SPECIALTIES	
Aviation Electrician's Mate	Aircraft Electrician, Electrical Product Repairer, Air Crew Member

Aviation Electronics Technician	Aircraft Electrician, Radio Equipment Repairer, Radar and Sonar Equipment Repairer, Electronic Instrument Repairer, Air Crew Member
Aviation Machinist Mate	Aircraft Mechanic, Machinist, Air Crew Member
Aviation Structural Mechanic	Aircraft Mechanic, Sheet Metal Worker, Machinist, Welder
Aviation Survivalman	Survival Equipment Specialist, Ordnance Mechanic, Air Crew Member

DECK AND ORDNANCE SPECIALTIES

Boatswain's Mate	Boat Operator, Heavy Equipment Operator
Fire Control Technician	Electrical Products Repairer, Electronic Weapons System Repairer, Radio Equipment Repairer, Radar and Sonar Equipment Repairer
Gunner's Mate	Ordnance Mechanic, Machinist, Artillery Crew Member
Quartermaster	Quartermaster, Boat Operator
Radarman	Radio Operator, Radar and Sonar Operator, Air Traffic Controller
Sonar Technician	Radar and Sonar Equipment Repairer, Radar and Sonar Operator

ENGINEERING AND HULL SPECIALTIES

Damage Controlman	Firefighter, Carpenter, Welder, Plumber and Pipefitter, Machinist
Electrician's Mate	Electrician, Telephone Technician, Teletype Repairer, Power Plant Electrician, Electrical Products Repairer
Electronics Technician	Radio Equipment Repairer, Electronic Instrument Repairer, Telephone Technician, Radar and Sonar Equipment Repairer, Radio Equipment Repairer, Data Processing Equipment Repairer
Machinery Technician	Automobile Mechanic, Heating and Cooling Mechanic, Shipfitter, Machinist
Telephone Technician	Telephone Technician, Teletype Repairer, Line Installer and Repairer, Radio Equipment Repairer, Telephone Operator, Teletype Operator

---

Note: Coast Guard ratings, like those of the Navy, are clusters of specialties. Individuals may work in one or all of these specialties during their career, or they may specialize in one or two of them.

Those who wish to enter Aviation ratings must pass an aircrew candidate physical examination and volunteer for duty involving flying in any type of Coast Guard aircraft.

Coast Guard Training

Coast Guard training begins with boot camp. Men attend boot camp at Cape May, New Jersey, or Alameda, California; boot camp for women is conducted only at Cape May. Boot camp lasts about eight weeks.

The training consists of a combination of physical conditioning, classroom work, and experience aboard small boats. Instruction is given in basic seamanship, marksmanship, radio communications, damage control, rescue techniques, and first aid. Coast Guard history, traditions, and customs are also studied.

Training for your Coast Guard occupational specialty follows boot camp. If you did not enlist under the Guaranteed School Program, you may be able to select a training field while you are attending boot camp; or you can wait until you are more familiar with the service and then request school training. The Coast Guard operates basic petty officer schools called Class A Schools for training in many specific specialties; the schools of other services are used for training in some special fields. Courses of instruction last from ten to forty-two weeks.

Coast Guard Training Centers are located at Governors Island, New York: Petaluma, California; Elizabeth City, North Carolina (aviation specialties); and Yorktown, Virgina. Training in radar, sonar, and fire control fields is provided by the Navy. Public Affairs trainees attend the Defense Information School at Fort Benjamin Harrison, Indiana. Health Services Technicians attend special courses at the Coast Guard Academy, New London, Connecticut.

Coast Guard trainees receive additional on-the-job training after they complete school courses. The technical training is generally sufficient to permit them to advance to the rank of Petty Officer Third Class (E-4) without further formal schooling.

Not all Coast Guard enlistees attend training schools. Those who do not are assigned to additional training at the Coast Guard Reserve Training Center, Yorktown, Virgina, or may "strike" for the rating on the job, under the supervision of experienced petty officers and with the aid of correspondence courses. These Seaman strikers are said to be in apprenticeship programs, but do not confuse this use of the term with the apprenticeship programs of the Department of Labor in other military services. The Coast Guard apprenticeships are in two fields: fireman and seaman, regardless of specialty.

Advanced technical training becomes available to career enlisted members of the Coast Guard. Class B and Class C schools prepare students for advanced petty officer ratings. The Coast Guard also offers training by correspondence through the Coast Guard Institute free of charge.

Advancement and Career Development

The Coast Guard rating system covers advancement from E-1 through E-9, with increasing responsibilities and opportunities for management experience. Coast Guard enlisted ranks are the same as those of the Navy. Although the ratings originally applied exclusively to petty officer ranks, E-4 and above, the term is now used interchangeably with military occupational specialty, since formal school training for the rating now can begin immediately after boot camp. The supplemental on-the-job training after technical school is still considered essential, however.

The Coast Guard Seaman Recruit (E-1) is promoted to Seaman Apprentice (E-2) when he or she completes recruit training. Promotion to Seaman (E-3) is based on time in grade (minimum of six months), demonstrated military and professional qualifications, completion of required correspondence courses, and recommendation of the commanding officer.

Promotion to Petty Officer ratings (E-4 through E-9) is based on the results of service-wide examinations for the rating in addition to all the requirements above.

U.S. COAST GUARD PHOTO

Rescue missions require courage

Enlisted members of the Coast Guard generally spend their career within the continental United States, mostly in assignments on the East Coast, Gulf Coast, and West Coast. Sea duty on a cutter may be part of the career experience; depending upon the rating, sea duty may be a major factor in a Coast Guard enlisted career. One or two tours of duty outside the United States are normal, as are out-of-specialty assignments such as recruiter.

Because of its mission and its small size, the Coast Guard offers exceptional opportunities to enlisted men and women to assume leadership roles early. The Coast Guard also encourages its members to further their education by attendance at a local college or university or by correspondence courses; the service pays one hundred percent of tuition costs, up to six credits each semester or quarter, depending upon the availability of funds. Senior Petty Officers in certain ratings can also compete for assignment to special degree programs in related areas.

An advanced electronics technology course leading to an associate degree is available to qualified enlisted personnel. Students who enter the program attend school full time in a resident status. Successful completion of the course qualifies the graduate for assignment as an Engineer's Assistant at Coast Guard Headquarters or other major headquarters and shore units. Engineer's Assistants are involved with the design of Coast Guard equipment.

Several Coast Guard programs provide opportunities for enlisted men and women to advance to officer status. These are discussed in the following section. Another program for Coast Guard enlisted members in the grades of E-6 and above qualifies them for direct appointment as Warrant Officer.

Another Warrant Officer program for enlisted men and women involves training to become a Physician's Assistant. This is a two-year full-time course of study at Duke University.

HOW TO BECOME A COAST GUARD OFFICER

The Coast Guard Academy at New London, Connecticut, is the primary source of career Coast Guard commissioned officers. Nearly ninety percent of Academy graduates remain on active duty beyond the required five years after graduation.

High school students who wish to attend the Academy must enter the nationwide competition held each year for the approximately three hundred spaces available in the freshman class. The Academy offers majors in civil, electrical, and marine engineering, applied science, mathematical and computer sciences, government, and management. Additional information is included in Chapter IV.

The Coast Guard also participates in the Navy's BOOST and Naval Academy Preparatory School programs; the objective is to prepare enlisted men and women to compete for selection by the Coast Guard Academy. These two programs are also described in Chapter IV.

The Coast Guard operates its own Officer Candidate School (OCS), at Yorktown, Virginia. Applications for the seventeen-week course are accepted from graduates of accredited colleges and universities.

Applicants for OCS must be citizens of the United States and between the ages of twenty-one and twenty-six. Those who have prior military service may use up to five years of their active-duty time to offset the upper age limit. Applicants are also required to obtain a qualifying score on the Officer Aptitude Rating examination.

Reserve commissions are awarded to graduates of Officer Candidate School, and each new officer is required to serve on active duty for three years. Duty assignments are based on the officer's educational background, experience, and stated preference but subject to the needs of the service. Many Coast Guard Reserve officers are integrated into the Regular service at the end of their obligatory tour of active duty under a continuing program designed to retain the best qualified OCS graduates in the Coast Guard.

A "temporary regular" commissioning program is available to career Coast Guard enlisted members in the grade of E-5 or above. Applicants may have as little as one year of college credit, though graduation from college is preferred. Training is conducted by the Coast Guard OCS. Graduates are awarded a commission that remains temporary until the officer is selected for promotion to Lieutenant. At that time the commission may be converted to a Regular Coast Guard Commission—subject, of course, to the needs of the service.

Several Coast Guard commissioning programs provide for the direct appointment of college and university graduates with skills, experience, or educational backgrounds needed by the service:

• Graduates of state or federal maritime academies can qualify for commissions up to Lieutenant Junior Grade; they serve for three years and are generally assigned to Marine Safety duties. Assignments in naval engineering are possible.

• Licensed officers of the merchant marine with at least two years' service may be commissioned in the grade of Lieutenant. On entering active duty, they are assigned duties in the Merchant Marine Safety Program, usually as inspectors, investigators, or licensing officers. Candidates must be under age thirty-eight.

• Graduate engineers with degrees in civil, electrical, or mechanical engineering or architecture may be commissioned in the Coast Guard Reserve in grades up to Lieutenant. Initial duty assignments are in the field of engineering. Officers in this category may be integrated into the regular Coast Guard after three years of commissioned service.

• Graduates of accredited law schools who have been admitted to the bar of a federal court or the highest court in a state may be commissioned as Lieutenant Junior Grade, Coast Guard Reserve. These officers serve three years on active duty as attorneys; assignments are to Coast Guard Headquarters or to District headquarters. Reserve commissions may be converted.

• Former military aviators from any military service may be eligible for direct appointment as Lieutenant Junior Grade and become Coast Guard aviators. They serve on active duty for three years, after which they may apply for extended active duty or integration into the regular officer ranks.

Officer Career Development

Coast Guard officers serve in a variety of assignments and perform a variety of duties in the "mission" fields discussed earlier. Women officers are eligible for a full range of assignments, including service aboard and eventual command of Coast Guard vessels.

Specializations are also available in such fields as personnel administration, naval engineering, financial management, supply management, data processing, communications management, and industrial management after initial duty assignments. Officers who have been integrated into the Regular Coast Guard are eligible for out-of-specialty assignments.

Because of the current reliance on aircraft for some of the functions that traditionally have been performed by ships, the Coast Guard has a great need for specially trained aviators. Officers on active duty can receive both basic and advanced flight training, usually at Naval Air Stations such as the one at Pensacola, Florida. The Coast Guard also operates its own flight training program for already qualified pilots; it concentrates on Coast Guard–specific operational training in both fixed-wing aircraft and helicopters. Women are not excluded from flying Coast Guard aircraft on operational missions, and many already do so.

Coast Guard officers are usually offered opportunities to attend civilian universities after about five years of commissioned service.

Fields of study are broad, though they are usually related to the officer's specialty.

Coast Guard officers also attend professional military schools operated by other services or the Department of Defense. Among them are the Armed Forces Staff College, the Navy Staff College, the National War College, and the Industrial College of the Armed Forces.

Service in the Coast Guard is demanding, if sometimes exciting, and is not for everyone. The officer corps is small but highly professional and oriented toward service. Officers and enlisted men and women alike are given important responsibilities early in their career. The high retention rate for Coast Guard Academy graduates and the zeal with which so many Coast Guard Reserve officers seek integration into the regular service seem to speak for themselves.

Chapter IX

The United States Air Force

The United States Air Force is the youngest of the five military services, having been formed only in 1947 when the former Army Air Corps was reorganized as a separate service.

The establishment of the United States Air Force occurred soon after the end of World War II, the first major conflict in which air power played a significant military role. Not incidentally, the birth of the new Air Force coincided with the beginning of the era of jet aircraft, the development of military rockets and missiles, and the exploration of space.

For all these reasons, perhaps, the United States Air Force has an image of a dynamic military organization operating at the leading edge of technology and considerably less bound by tradition than the other services. And, indeed, the Air Force does seem to have an imaginative, "can do" approach to military plans and operations that has at times startled and even angered the more conservative representatives of the older services.

The image persists from top to bottom, fostered by the seemingly deliberate efforts of senior Air Force policymakers to promote the idea of youth and vitality.

The sudden appearance, in the early 1950s, of officers and airmen alike clad in the now-traditional "Air Force Blue" uniforms wiped out the casual image that the old Army Air Corps had enjoyed. The jaunty "Fifty Mission Crush" that distinguished the olive drab felt caps of Air Corps pilots from those of the Army's ground officers was discarded, along with the cap. Officers and enlisted men alike were now issued crisply correct powder-blue gabardine visored caps decorated with silver eagles, the latter another distinct departure from the gold eagles that had graced the caps of generations of Army officers.

The new Air Force also discarded the "pinks and greens" of the Army officer's Class A uniform in favor of a tailored blue uniform that recalled those of the British Royal Air Force—and then had the nerve to dress Air Force enlisted members in the same uniform. Even the shoes prescribed for the new uniforms were black, at a time when the Army, the Navy, and the Marines were still clumping around in plain brown brogans.

The Air Force retained the traditional bars, leaves, eagles, and stars that denoted officer ranks, but turned the old Army chevrons of enlisted ranks upside down, changed the colors to blue and silver, and added a silver star in a blue circle at the apex of the stripes. The first four enlisted grades were redesignated Airman Basic, Airman, Airman First Class, and Senior Airman, doing away with the former ranks of Private, Private First Class, and Corporal of the Army Air Corps. The new enlisted classification system also did away with the confusion of specialist and line designations that still plagues the Army.

The new look was greeted with polite amusement by the olive drab-clad members of the Army, many of whom seemed to derive great pleasure from labeling the men in blue Greyhound bus drivers.

But the grins slowly faded as the startlingly contemporary buildings of the new Air Force Academy rose in the dramatic foothills of the Rocky Mountains, far away in Colorado from the ivy-clad gothic towers of the historic Military Academy at West Point. The differences did not end with the architecture: the new Air Force Academy quickly became one of the great educational institutions of the United States.

The construction of the Academy was paralleled by construction of modern quarters for enlisted members of the Air Force at a time when the Army's enlisted personnel were still largely housed in open barracks.

Meanwhile, the new service quickly staked out its turf. The Air Force pioneered the flashy "jet age"; built up the innovative Strategic Air Force; secured a firm grip on missile warfare (at one time, anything that flew through the air farther than a 155 mm artillery shell seemed to be claimed by the Air Force); cornered a major portion of the nuclear weapons field; loaded the fledgling astronaut program with Air Force test pilots; and established a presumably impregnable system for the defense of the United States and Canada from attack by air.

In recent years the Air Force has been busy lobbying for production of the long-overdue B-1 bomber, campaigning for the controversial MX missile, establishing a Space Command to control military satellites, and backing the space-based "Star Wars" antiballistic misile defense project, among other things.

The glamour associated with the United States Air Force has worked wonders. For one thing, the Air Force can now claim to be close to its goal that every new enlisted member should be a high school graduate and every officer a graduate of an accredited four-year college or university. By the end of 1984, ninety-nine percent of all new Air Force recruits had the high school diploma.

Moreover, the reenlistment rate for first-term enlisted members of the Air Force is the highest for the military services, as is the retention rate for career non-commissioned officers. The Air Force also has the greatest ratio of females to males of the armed services: women make up about eleven percent of all enlisted members and about twelve percent of officers. Women in the Air Force perform in just about every Air Force occupation, including flying military aircraft.

Ironically, the high retention rate means that the Air Force is no longer quite so "young" as it was forty-odd years ago when nineteen-year-old fighter pilots gained control of the air space over Hitler's Europe and twenty-five-year-old colonels commanded big bomber units. Furthermore, a startling sixty-three percent of all Air Force personnel are married; the number of spouses, children, and other dependents of Air Force members exceeds the total strength of the service by nearly half.

As the years go by, tradition is perhaps beginning to catch up with the Air Force. The exploits of the half-forgotten pioneers of military aviation, the aerial campaigns of World War II and the flying aces for whom the Air Force has named its major airbases and other installations are now the subject of lessons in military history for new recruits and would-be officers.

In particular, I recall the circumstances of an old friend of mine who was the proud but dimly remembered pilot of the B-26 bomber that flew the greatest number of missions over Europe during World War II. The front half of the fuselage of the aircraft, with the names of the original crew still stenciled on it, is enshrined in the Air and Space Museum in Washington. Over the past ten years or so, a great cult has grown up around "Flak Bait" and its surviving crew members. The cultists are not, however, graying veterans of the war; they are much younger students of the history of aerial warfare. Of such stuff are traditions made.

ORGANIZATION AND MISSIONS OF THE AIR FORCE

The United States Air Force, like the other military services, has as its primary mission the defense of the United States and its interests, at home and abroad. During the forty years since the Air Force was established as a separate military service within the Department of

Defense, this mission has been broken into a number of components. Among other things, the Air Force must:

1. Organize, equip, and train necessary forces for prompt and sustained air operations, including defending the United States against air attack, gaining and maintaining aerial supremacy (locally or generally), defeating enemy air forces, and participating in joint amphibious and airborne operations.
2. Organize, equip, and train forces for strategic air warfare, including development, procuring, and operating air defense surface-to-air missile (SAM) systems with ranges greater than one hundred miles, surface-to-surface missiles (SAS) with ranges greater than 400 miles, intermediate range ballistic missiles (IRBM) with ranges of 500 to 1,500 miles, and intercontinental ballistic missiles (ICBM).
3. Support combat operations of the United States Army, including airborne operations, by providing airlift from points outside the combat zone for supplies, equipment, personnel, and units, by providing aerial reconnaissance, by providing close-in combat support to Army ground forces, by destroying enemy installations behind the lines, by interrupting enemy lines of communication, and by providing air evacuation of troops, supplies, and equipment.

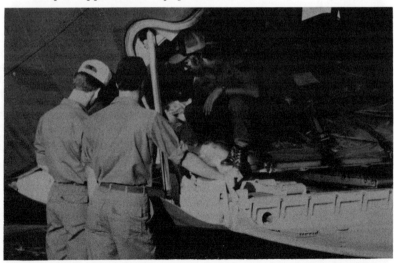

Air Force technicians check equipment

4. Support the United States Navy, as required, to protect shipping, to interdict enemy naval forces, to conduct anti-submarine warfare, and to lay mines.

The United States Air Force now maintains an active force of about 600,000 uniformed personnel, the second-largest American military force after the Army. The Air Force also has a reserve pool of about 255,000 men and women, some of whom are used on a day-to-day basis to assist the active Air Force, particularly with air transportation around the world. Air Force Reserve pilots and air crews keep their flying skills at an operational level; and the active Air Force can concentrate on other things.

The principal aerial weapons available to the Air Force are about 1,850 interceptor, attack, and fighter-bomber aircraft, 300 strategic bombers, 535 cargo aircraft, 45 flying tankers, and 1,000 land-based ICBMs.

Nearly three fourths of all active Air Force people are located in the continental United States, but large numbers are stationed at advanced bases and other installations in Alaska, Hawaii, and Guam. The largest concentrations of Air Force personnel outside the United States and its territories are in Western and Southern Europe (especially in West Germany, the United Kingdom, Italy, Greece, and Turkey), in East Asia (Japan, Korea, and the Philippines), and in Panama.

Headquarters U.S. Air Force

The management of the Department of the Air Force is the responsibility of the Secretary of the Air Force, a civilian appointed by the President of the United States. He is also specifically responsible for the direction and supervision of Air Force space programs and activities.

The Chief of Staff of the Air Force, a four-star general, is the principal military adviser to the Secretary and his civilian assistants. He is responsible for operational planning, training and equipping the operating forces, and the everyday operations and administration of the Air Force. The Chief of Staff also represents the Air Force as a member of the Joint Chiefs of Staff, in the Department of Defense. He is assisted by a Vice Chief of Staff and an Assistant Vice Chief of Staff, who coordinate policy matters and supervise the work of the Air Staff.

The Air Staff is made up of a number of Deputy Chiefs of Staff, each of whom is responsible for a functional area such as manpower and personnel, research and development, logistics and engineering, and operational planning. Other technical advisers, including the Surgeon General, the Judge Advocate General, the Chaplain, the Chief of Air Force Reserves, and the Assistant Chief of Staff for Intelligence, report directly to the Chief of Staff.

Major Air Commands

The operating forces of the Air Force are distributed through a dozen or so major Air Force commands. For purposes of this chapter, these commands have been classed as operational commands and supporting commands. Operational commands are those with combat or other operational missions. In the list that follows, the abbreviation "AFB" stands for Air Force Base.

Operational Commands
Alaskan Air Command	Elmendorf AFB, Alaska
Military Airlift Command	Scott AFB, Illinois
Pacific Air Forces	Hickam AFB, Hawaii
Space Command	Colorado Springs, Colorado
Strategic Air Command (SAC)	Offutt AFB, Nebraska
Tactical Air Command (TAC)	Langley AFB, Virginia
U.S. Air Forces, Europe	Ramstein AFB, Germany

Supporting Commands
Air Force Communications Command	Scott AFB, Illinois
Air Force Logistics Command	Wright-Patterson AFB, Ohio
Air Force Systems Command	Andrews AFB, Maryland
Air Training Command	Randolph AFB, Texas
Electronic Security Command	San Antonio, Texas
The Air University	Maxwell AFB, Alabama

The Air Force organization also includes a number of separate operating agencies that provide centralized services in such fields as accounting and finance, personnel, automatic data processing, special investigations, health services, intelligence, and operational testing and evaluation.

ENLISTING IN THE AIR FORCE

Initial enlistment in the United States Air Force is for four or six years. Men and women between the ages of seventeen and twenty-seven who are U.S. citizens or resident aliens are eligible to apply.

The usual other requirements also apply: good physical and mental health, good moral character, and a high school diploma.

Although most new recruits are high school graduates, the Air Force allows outstanding applicants who have not completed high school to delay entry for up to a year while they finish. Because of the competition for the 60,000 new Air Force slots each year, superior academic credentials are almost a necessity, along with good performance on the Armed Services Vocational Aptitude Battery (ASVAB).

Air Force Enlistment Options

Most Air Force enlisted men and women enter the service under one of the two principal enlistment programs: the Guaranteed Training Enlistment Program (GTEP) and the Aptitude Area Enlistment Program (AAEP)

Several options are available under the GTEP. In general, qualified applicants who enlist for four years may choose from among more than 150 Air Force specialties and be guaranteed, in writing, training and a job assignment in that specialty. Air Force occupations include almost all those listed in Appendix C with the exception of some combat specialties (infantry, armor, artillery), though Special Forces specialties are included.

Those who enlist for six years may select from about 70 skill fields; they are assured of promotion to Airman First Class upon completion of basic training. In some cases, six-year enlistees may also be guaranteed retraining in another skill field halfway through the enlistment, providing the enlistee qualifies and a vacancy exists.

Other options under the GTEP include:

1. Enlistment as Airman First Class (E-3). This option is available to:
   a. enlistees who have successfully completed a three-year Junior ROTC program or who have received the Billy Mitchell or higher award for participation in the Civil Air Patrol program; and,
   b. applicants who have accumulated a minimum of 45 semester hours of college credit (67 quarter hours).
2. Accelerated Promotion to Airman (E-2), available to:
   a. four-year enlistees who qualify for training in critically needed skills; promotion to E-2 follows basic training;
   b. applicants with at least 20 semester hours (30 quarter hours) of college credit.

3. Enlistment Bonuses: Available to enlistees who qualify in certain designated skill areas; bonuses of $1,000 to $2,000 are paid upon completion of basic training.

The AAEP permits qualified applicants to select from one of four career areas (administration, electronics, mechanical, and general), based on their ASVAB scores. Actual job selection or assignment takes place during basic training. According to the Air Force, the factors that influence job assignments are ASVAB scores, civilian education and experience, personal interests, and needs of the service—not necessarily in that order.

Anyone enlisting under the Aptitude Area program may be taking a large calculated risk. Scores in the various aptitude areas are used, in part, to determine assignment potentials. But strange jobs are included in the Electronics area: cooks and bakers, firefighters, truck drivers, and most medical service specialties—all at or near the lower end of the spectrum of ASVAB scores, which is to say, under 45.

If you have your heart set on training in Electronics and got your best ASVAB score in that Aptitude Area (let's say the score was around 45), be sure to ask for the list of jobs currently open in the area before you sign on the dotted line. Some very good electronics specialties are indeed available in that score range; but not many. The best jobs in Electronics require ASVAB scores in the upper 60s.

On the other hand, if you got an Electronics score of 45 on the preliminary ASVAB that you took at your high school, you may be able to upgrade your standing means of special courses, by taking some tutoring, or by boning up on your own before you take the ASVAB again for purposes of enlisting in the Air Force.

Of course, there is nothing wrong with being a cook or a firefighter or a veterinary specialist, but those jobs do not have much to do with electronics.

As a general rule for anyone interested in the Air Force, you should probably check Appendix C to determine the range of ASVAB scores suggested for the occupational field or fields of your choice. Next, sign up for the ASVAB while you are still in school. When you get your scores, match them against those suggested for the occupational specialties you selected. If you did not do well enough to qualify, get out the books and study!

Note, of course, that the range of ASVAB scores for each occupation shown in Appendix C is at the high end of the scale. If your scores are in that range, you should have a 90 to 95 percent chance of qualifying for Air Force training in the specializations that interest you most.

Training to Be a Member of the Air Force

After the preenlistment processing has been completed and you have taken the enlistment oath, you are sent to Lackland Air Force Base, near San Antonio, Texas, for six weeks of recruit training. Air Force basic training is intended to provide a necessary transition from civilian to military life and is similar in instructional content and emphasis on drill and physical conditioning to the recruit training provided by other services. The duration of basic training in the Air Force is somewhat shorter, but it would be a mistake to conclude that it is any less rigorous than that of the other services.

During basic training, enlistees who have entered under the AAEP receive orientation and individual counseling to help them choose a job specialty. If you do not have a guarantee for a specific training program, this is where the term "needs of the service" may come into play.

To go back to the earlier discussion, you may have selected Electronics as your enlistment option despite your score of only 45 on the ASVAB; you hope to become a computer operator. At your interview, however, you are told that no job openings are available for computer operators. Your Classifier tells you that the only jobs available in Electronics are (1) Electrician, (2) Truck Driver, and (3) Food Service Specialist. You gulp and wonder why you didn't study harder before you took the ASVAB at the Military Processing Center.

Regardless of the enlistment option you selected during the recuiting period, you will be expected to perform at your best once you enter the Air Force. Basic training separates the men from the boys and the women from the girls; if you cannot keep up, you may even be discharged from the service. On the other hand, if you are as good as you (and your Recruiter) think you are, you will have few real problems during basic training. And, even though you may wonder at times why you enlisted, you will probably be a better person for the experience.

ENLISTED CAREER DEVELOPMENT

Technical training follows completion of basic training. Most graduates are sent to formal technical schools operated by the Air Training Command. Resident courses last from a few weeks to several months, but each course is designed to provide the basic skills and knowledge necessary to the performance of the first assignment in the specialty.

Air Force technical training centers are located at Chanute AFB, Illinois; Keesler AFB, Mississippi; Lackland AFB, Texas: Lowry AFB, Colorado; Sheppard AFB and Goodfellow AFB, both in Texas, and elsewhere.

Air Force enlistees who are not sent immediately to a Technical Training Center usually go directly to their first job assignment, where they receive on-the-job training in their skill field.

On-the-job training is an organized, two-part program consisting of supervised job performance and study. Typically, Airmen either study Air Force technical manuals or enroll in skill-related correspondence courses. They work under trainers and supervisors, who observe them and guide them in the performance of their assigned tasks.

Every skill field has its own career development pattern leading from entry-level jobs to supervisory positions. Advanced training in the skill field is provided along the route.

Advancement in the Air Force

Promotions through the pay grade of E-3 (Airman First Class) are noncompetitive and usually depend only upon the recommendation of the commanding officer.

Airman Basic (E-1) is the customary enlisted entry grade; promotion to Airman (E-2) usually occurs after about six months of service. Airmen may be promoted to Airman First Class (E-3) within about twelve to sixteen months of total service, and after six months in grade.

Exceptions to this pattern apply to those who enlist under programs that offer accelerated promotions. Graduates of Junior ROTC programs or recruits who enlist under the Stripes for College program, for example, are promoted upon completion of basic training.

Promotion to Senior Airman (E-4) is also noncompetitive and normally occurs after thirty to thirty-six months of Air Force service, by which time enlisted members are considered to be fully qualified in their specialty. A special program allows outstanding Airmen First Class to be promoted earlier. Earlier promotion to E-4 can also be the result of enlistment in the accelerated promotion programs already mentioned.

Interestingly, the Air Force has two different enlisted ranks at the pay grade of E-4: Senior Airman and Sergeant. While promotion to E-4 in most other military services confers Non-Commissioned Officer status, a Senior Airman in the Air Force is not in that category. Appointment to the rank of Sergeant (E-4) does carry

NCO status, but that step requires an additional year of service after becoming a Senior Airman. During that year, the Senior Airman is required to complete an introductory Professional Military Education Course that prepares him or her for leadership and management assignments.

Considering the provisions for accelerated promotions, a well-qualified enlisted man or woman in the Air Force could become a Senior Airman within eighteen months and be promoted to Sergeant in the middle of his or her third year of service.

Promotions to the rank of Staff Sergeant (E-5), Technical Sergeant (E-6), Master Sergeant (E-7), and above are very competitive in the Air Force. Eligible candidates compete with all others around the world who hold the same grade and military occupational specialty.

Actual promotion is based on a number of factors: time in grade and total years of service, test scores, performance ratings, commendations and awards, among others. Promotion scores developed at the Headquarters USAF level are made available to those eligible for promotion to show them where they stand compared to others in the same specialty and where improvement may be needed.

Meanwhile, these Air Force non-commissioned officers develop leadership and management skills at NCO academies, under the Professional Military Education program, and are increasingly utilized in management and leadership roles. They may become instructors at one of the Technical Training Centers, be assigned to Air Force ROTC units or duty with Air Force Reserve or Air Force National Guard organizations, serve on the staffs of Air Force and joint commands, or be assigned abroad as military advisers or to serve military attaché duty at American Embassies. On the way up the career ladder, many Air Force NCOs complete requirements for college degrees.

Enlisted men and women who advance to the senior NCO grades of Senior Master Sergeant (E-8) and Chief Master Sergeant (E-9) have great responsibilities and much prestige in the Air Force as managers and highly qualified experts in their technical fields.

Educational Opportunities

The Air Force offers enlisted members many educational opportunities. These include award of college credits for technical training, earning college credit by examination, and tuition assistance for those who attend on-base off-duty college courses in degree programs.

The Air Force Bootstrap program assigns enlisted men and women on "temporary duty" for up to one year to civilian colleges and universities to enable them to complete degree requirements.

Candidates are usually selected from among senior NCOs, who may have accumulated a great many college credits during their service. Students under this program continue to receive the full pay and allowances of their Air Force grade. Some Bootstrap graduates attend Officer Training School and earn commissions as Air Force officers.

Well-qualified enlisted men and women with less service may apply for the Air Force Academy Preparatory School. Attendance at the preparatory school is designed to improve academic qualifications (emphasis on English, math, science) and prepare candidates physically and mentally to qualify for appointment to the Air Force Academy. Additional details about this program may be found in Chapter IV.

BECOMING AN OFFICER IN THE UNITED STATES AIR FORCE

The sources of newly commissioned officers in recent years show that the Air Force is close to realizing its goal that every commissioned officer should be at least a college graduate. More than half of these new officers come directly from four-year colleges and universities, including the Air Force Academy (about 11 percent) and the schools affiliated with the Air Force ROTC program (43 percent). Another large group of university graduates and postgraduates (14 percent) received direct commissions in the Air Force because of their academic and professional accomplishments. The remainder of the new officers entered the ranks from the Officer Training School program (27 percent).

Training for aviation careers is available to selected graduates of the three principal commissioning programs: the USAF Academy, the AFROTC program, and Officer Training School. Candidates for aviation training (pilot or navigator) must meet special age requirements and make a satisfactory score on the Air Force Officer Qualification Test. As you know by now, of course, not all Air Force officers are pilots and navigators. The other career options are many and varied.

Unlike the other military services, the Air Force has no Warrant Officer category.

How to Qualify for a Commission

The pathways to commissioned officer status in the Air Force are similar to those of the Army and the Navy. The Air Force has, however, a direct appointment program for professionals that is

U.S. AIR FORCE PHOTO

Air Force engineers prepare roadbed

somewhat broader than that of the other two services. The requirements for each commissioning method are as follows.

1. *United States Air Force Academy.* The Air Force Academy at Colorado Springs, Colorado, offers an excellent four-year college program to selected high school graduates, including both civilians and recently graduated enlisted men and women serving on active duty with the Air Force. Tuition is free; the Air Force also provides board and room, uniforms, books and supplies, and an allowance of about five hundred dollars a month to students, who are known as cadets.

Each year about 1,500 appointments as cadets are available, but the selection process is highly competitive. High school students should apply during their junior year. Graduates of the Air Force Academy are commissioned as Second Lieutenants in the Air Force and form the nucleus of the career officer corps. They must serve on active duty a minimum of five years. Chapter IV gives additional details about entrance requirements and application procedures.

2. *Air Force Reserve Officers Training Program (AFROTC)*. Commissioning through participation in the AFROTC is open to qualified men and women who are full-time students at one of about one hundred and fifty colleges and universities that host an AFROTC unit, and to several hundred associated institutions. Completion of the four-year AFROTC program results in a commission as a Second Lieutenant, U.S. Air Force Reserve. Graduates are obligated to serve on active duty for at least four years.

The military instruction under the ROTC program is presented over the entire four years of the college program, but qualified students may complete the program in the final two years of their university studies under certain conditions. Credit for some or all of the military instruction normally presented during the first two years may be allowed students who have completed two or more years of Junior ROTC training (high school level), have participated in the Civil Air Patrol program, or have had prior military service.

Any qualified student may enter the AFROTC General Military Program as a college freshman simply by registering for ROTC when registering for other college courses. No military obligation is involved during the first two years. Students enrolled in the AFROTC General Military Program receive uniforms and textbooks required for their military courses; they receive no pay or allowances.

Entry into the final two years of the training, called the Professional Officer Course, is competitive. Applicants who are accepted are enlisted in the Air Force Reserve and receive allowances of one hundred dollars a month (during the school year), uniforms, and necessary books and supplies. Cadets who are qualified for pilot training attend a flight indoctrination course during the senior year.

Successful ROTC candidates are commissioned Second Lieutenants in the United States Air Force upon graduation from college. Candidates who elect nonflying options must serve four years on active duty. Candidates who enter and complete flight training have additional obligations: four years after receiving their rating, for Navigators; five years after certification, for Pilots.

The Air ROTC program also offers scholarships that cover the costs of tuition and fees, textbooks, and uniforms for students who enroll in certain technical degree programs. About 1,500 such scholarships are available each year; terms of the scholarships vary from two to four years.

Scholarship applicants must be able to complete all requirements for a commission by age 25, unless they have had prior military service (age limit at commissioning is 29). Nonscholarship students must complete commissioning requirements before they reach age 30 (age 35, if prior service). Exceptions to these requirements may apply in the case of students who elect aviation options.

A special program is available for nursing students who have completed two years at an accredited nursing school with a grade point average of 2.5. Qualified students may be awarded scholarships and a subsistence allowance of one hundred dollars a month. They are commissioned Second Lieutenants upon completion of the program.

Prospective medical students who are enrolled in an AFROTC program may qualify for full scholarship to medical school under the Air Force Pre-Health Professions Program. Approved applicants are guaranteed an Armed Forces Health Professions Scholarship to attend the medical school of their choice. The scholarships pay all tuition and fees and provide a monthly stipend of $530 a month during the academic year.

The Armed Forces Health Professions Scholarship recipients are commissioned Second Lieutenants upon completion of their ROTC program and graduation from college, but they are not required to report for active duty until they have graduated from medical school. During their medical studies, scholarship holders perform 45 days of active duty each year, for which they receive the full pay and allowances of their rank. Scholarship recipients must serve on active duty for six years following graduation from medical school. Candidates are usually promoted to the rank of First Lieutenant when they are called to active duty (internship); they may be promoted to Captain at the end of their internship in an Air Force or other military medical facility.

Another special ROTC program is available to Airmen on active duty with the Air Force. Scholarships are provided for two to four years, depending upon the college credits already accumulated. The terms are the same as for other ROTC scholarships: full tuition and fees, textbooks, uniforms, and allowances of one hundred dollars a month during the academic year. Airmen who are awarded ROTC scholarships are transferred to the Air Force Reserve while they attend college. Commissions are awarded upon completion of ROTC training and all requirements for the bachelor's degree; the active-duty obligation is four years. This program is reported to be highly competitive.

3. *Officer Training School*. Male and female graduates of accredited four-year colleges may apply to attend Officer Training School, a twelve-week course conducted at Lackland Air Force Base, near San Antonio, Texas. Applicants should be between the ages of twenty and a half (20-½) years and twenty-nine and a half (29-½)

years and able to earn a commission before their thirtieth birthday. Applicant who is also a candidate for flight training must be able to complete commissioning requirements and enter flight training before reaching the age of twenty-seven and a half (27-½). Applicants must also make a satisfactory score on the Air Force Officer Qualification Test.

Approved candidates are enlisted in the Air Force Reserve, as Officer Candidates, for four years. Upon entering the Officer Training School program, they are promoted to the rank of Staff Sergeant (E-5); during the program, they are paid at that grade. Commissions as Second Lieutenants are awarded to those who complete the course. Newly commissioned officers scheduled for flight training remain at Lackland AFB for three weeks of primary flight training, unless they are already licensed as private pilots.

Nonflying officer graduates of the Officer Training School serve on active duty for four years after commissioning. Officers who complete flight training incur additional active-duty obligations. Navigators serve for five years after receiving their rating; pilots, for six years.

4. *Direct Appointments.* The Air Force offers qualified professionals opportunities for direct appointments as officers, without any previous officer training. Most of these direct appointments are tendered to those in the medical and health fields; the exceptions are chaplains and lawyers.

a. Physicians and Dentists. Must be graduates of accredited medical or dental schools accepted by the Surgeon General with internships completed (physicians) or at least one year of practice (dentists). Age limits vary. Minimum appointment is First Lieutenant; generally serve on active duty in grade of Captain or above, depending upon experience. Service obligation: three years.

b. Nurses. Graduates of accredited, approved nursing schools who are fully licensed in the United States or its possessions may be appointed as Second Lieutenants or First Lieutenants, depending upon experience. Age limitation vary. Service obligation: three years.

c. Medical Service Corps. Graduates in fields of hospital or health care administration and management, with a minimum of BA/BS degree, may be appointed as Second Lieutenants. Those with advanced degree and/or experience may be commissioned at higher grades. Service obligation: three years.

d. Biomedical Sciences. Applicants must have a degree or a certificate appropriate to the specialty from an institution approved by the Surgeon General. Commissions in the Air Force Reserve are offered; grades depend upon training, experience, and age. Active-duty obligation: three years (voluntary). Fields included: pharmacy, dietetics, physical therapy, occupational therapy, biomedical laboratory specialties, medical entomology, health physics, clinical social work, optometry, podiatry, aerospace physiology, bioenvironmental engineering, audiology, speech therapy.

e. Chaplains. Applicants must hold the degree of Master of Divinity or equivalent, be ordained and actively engaged in the ministry, and endorsed by the religious organization. Age: up to 42 years. Commissioned in the Air Force Reserve (grade varies). Active-duty obligation: three years (voluntary).

Another Chaplain program is available for applicants under age thirty who have a college degree and are enrolled in a recognized seminary; with ecclesiastical approval, applicants may be commissioned Second Lieutenants, USAFR; they attend the Air Force Chaplains School between seminary terms, with full pay. Upon graduation, they are promoted to First Lieutenants and may volunteer to serve on active duty as Air Force Chaplains for three years.

f. Lawyers: Graduates of law schools accredited by the American Bar Association and who are admitted to the bar of a federal court or the highest court in a state may be commissioned First Lieutenants. Age limits: 22 to 33; waivers up to age 36. Service obligation: four years.

OFFICER CAREER FIELDS

The complexity of the Air Force and its missions suggests that officer career fields should be many and varied, and that is exactly the situation. More than thirty major career areas have been developed; some have several subspecialties. An abbreviated list is given below, based on Air Force Regulation 36-1.

OFFICER CAREER FIELDS

Career Area	Code	Specializations
International Political-Military Affairs		
Disaster Preparedness		
Operations		
	10–13	Pilots
	14	Air Operations Officer
	15	Navigator
	16	Air Traffic Controller
	17	Air Weapons Director
	18	Missile Operations Officer
	20	Space Operations Officer
	21	Navigator, Air Operations

Audiovisual	23	
Weather	25	
Science and Development		
Engineering	26	Scientific
	27	Aquisitions Program Management
	28	Development Engineering
Program Management	29	Program Management
Logistics	31	Missile Maintenance
	40	Aircraft Maintenance
Information Systems	49	
Civil Engineering	55	
Cartography and Geodesy	57	
Logistics		
	60	Transportation
	62	Services
	64	Supply Management
	65	Acquisition Contracting and Manufacturing
	66	Logistics Plans and Programs
Comptroller		
	67	Financial
	69	Cost and Management Analysis
Personnel Resources		
Management	70	Administration
	73	Personnel
	74	Manpower Management
	75	Education and Training
Public Affairs	79	
Intelligence	80	
Security Police	81	
Special Investigations	82	
Band	87	
Legal	88	
Chaplain	89	
Medical		
Health Services Management	90	
Biomedical Sciences	91, 92	
Physicians	93–94	
Nurses	97	
Dental	98	
Veterinary	99	

Officer Career Development

Guidelines for each Air Force specialty provide for a career of twenty to thirty years, with assignments to ensure command experience as well as familiarity with operations, administration, and technical functions in the Air Force.

Officers in flight specialties are usually utilized for at least five years in the Operations career area. Because such experience influences programs and operation in other Air Force fields, flight-trained officers may then be given assignments in such fields as intelligence, maintenance, and development engineering, for example.

Nonrated (nonflying) Air Force officers usually progress through their initial specialty area, though changes in specialty may be made as well as assignments outside the specialty.

A typical career development pattern might include a period for initial development of technical and leadership skills (years 0 to 3), an intermediate development phase during years 4 to 7 (possible attendance at the Air Force Institute of Technology in this period); and a period for advanced development during years 8 to 15, with at least some command experience. These phases may be equated, in general, to officer ranks.

Initial development: 2nd Lieutenant–1st Lieutenant

Intermediate development: Captain

Advanced development: Captain to Major (possibly to Lt. Colonel).

During these three career phases, Air Force officers in the grades of 1st Lieutenant and Captain probably attend professional development courses at the Squadron Officer School. Some officers in the grade of Captain and Major are selected to attend the Air Command and Staff College during the Advanced Development phase.

The three development phases are followed by utilization phases that involve more advanced and responsible staff and command assignments for officers in the grades of Major, Lieutenant Colonel, and Colonel. During these phases, some officers are selected to attend the Air War College or other sister-service colleges of the same type.

The prospects for a fruitful career in the United States Air Force remain bright whether or not you want to fly a jet fighter through the sound barrier. Not too many years ago, pilots in the Air Force seemed to receive preferential treatment in military education, staff and command assignments, and promotions, but this is no longer the case. Pilots are still the backbone of the Air Force, but the service has adopted so many nonflying operational programs and projects in the past forty years that they may not be so forever. Unmanned atmospheric and space vehicles and weapons have caught the attention of the Air Force. Thus we could conclude this chapter by saying that, for the Air Force, the sky is no longer the limit.

CONSIDERATIONS FOR MILITARY CAREER PLANNING

Introduction

The information in Part III is just as essential as that in the previous chapters, though the emphasis is somewhat different. Until now, we have been concerned largely with the aspects of military service that make it an attractive career. We have concentrated on the qualifications you need to enter military service. We have suggested some of the ways in which you can make the military services work for you, whether you plan a full career or simply want to take advantage of the excellent occupational training and educational opportunities the services offer. And we have explored some of the circumstances of career development in the five military services that can make your term of service a rewarding one.

The fact is, however, that few young men and women who enter military service spend their entire adult life in uniform. And that fact is extremely important in career planning: In general, everyone who serves in a military service is, in one form or another, a citizen soldier. The majority of those now serving in uniform leave active service after the first tour of duty for one reason or another. Even those who elect to pursue military careers generally serve only for about twenty years on active duty, though some may serve for up to thirty years—and even longer, in a few exceptional cases—before they are forced to retire to civilian life.

This means that you may be out of the service—perhaps with retirement pay—and back in the civilian workplace at some time during your productive years. If you enlist in the Army at age eighteen, for example, you could under current law be eligible to "retire" when you are thirty-eight years old, an age when many of your civilian counterparts have barely reached mid-career. If you did not complete the years of service required for military retirement, you may enter the civilian work force under difficult circumstances unless you have done some realistic career planning.

The purpose of these two chapters, therefore, is to explore with you the conditions of life in military service and what you may expect when you leave. Chapter X discusses some of the nonduty aspects of life in military service, including some of the advantages and disadvantages, and outlines some of the benefits that you may gain whether or not you make it your career. In Chapter XI the focus is on ways in which the armed forces Reserves may be important to you, either as an alternative to an active military career or as a means to augment a short term of military service or an interrupted active-duty career.

Chapter **X**

Your Life in Military Service and Beyond

No one can possibly tell you in advance what your life in military service will be like. In the first place, the conditions and quality of the "military life" differ from service to service and even from assignment to assignment. You can easily imagine that your life-style as a career infantry officer in the Army would be quite different from that of a machinist's mate in the Navy's submarine service or a data processing specialist in the Air Force. Moreover, how you live your life after you have made a few basic decisions is pretty much up to you, in the military as in any other part of our society. What we can do in this chapter is to help you understand the similarities and differences of military and civilian life-styles so that you will be better prepared for what seems to be meant when people use the term "military life."

We have already discussed some of the factors that govern military service and some of the opportunities it offers. In this section we shall examine broader aspects of military service as they may affect you over a period of years. This chapter reviews the basic benefits and privileges of military service, discusses opportunities for professional and personal development with a focus on off-duty activities, examines some aspects of family life in military service, and outlines problems and prospects that may face you when you leave. Details are sketchy, of necessity, but you should be able to reach an informed opinion about whether you should seek a career in military service or enter for only a limited time to pursue some personal objective such as training for a technical career.

HAVING THE "RIGHT STUFF"

Perhaps the first thing to do before looking at the advantages and disadvantages of life in the military is to take a good look at yourself. Do you have what it takes to make the most of the opportunities that military service can offer you without coming apart at the seams when you are faced with some obstacle or other? Or perhaps the better question is: "How do I know what it takes?"

General John Wickham, then Army Chief of Staff, wrote an article entitled "Soldier Values" for the November 1985 issue of the Army publication *Soldiers* that seems to strike the right note for members of all the military services. General Wickham, a West Point graduate with more than thirty years of active Army service behind him, first summarized what he called the "Army ethic." He then went on to discuss the personal values essential to a successful Army career. For our purposes, let's assume that he was discussing the military services as a whole and military careers in general.

General Wickham cited four fundamental values in the "Army ethic": loyalty to the institution, loyalty to the military unit, personal responsibility, and selfless service. What did he mean by those terms?

Loyalty to the institution means, first of all, loyalty to the nation and what it stands for; it also means loyalty to the military service. New members of all services pledge that loyalty when they take the enlistment oath or oath of office.

Loyalty to the unit involves the responsibility of every member of a military service to serve as a member of a team. Of course, loyalty in this sense works in both directions: from the top down, as well as from the bottom up.

Personal responsibility, General Wickham wrote, means that every service member, including military leaders, must take responsibility for his or her actions and endeavor to do "what is right," ethically and morally as well as professionally.

Selfless service grows out of the other three values. The best interests of the nation, the military service, and the military unit determine "what is right," not a drive for personal gain. Put another way, the military "mission" is usually the factor that dictates individual performance.

Especially important to anyone who is even considering a military career is General Wickham's discussion of the "four Cs." They summarize the personal values essential to a military career: *commitment* (to service), *competence* (on the job), *candor* (with yourself as well as with others), and *courage* (both moral and physical). The development of the "four Cs" in individuals is the objective of military training, and the demonstration of these qualities is what distinguishes career members of the military services as professionals.

None of this means, however, that military service smothers individual initiative or deliberately frustrates personal goals and objectives. Rather, the conditions of military service place great emphasis on the development of self-discipline, character-building, team play, and behavior oriented to the common good without sacrificing the factor of individual choice. Army Sergeant Donnie Hall summed it all up in a letter to the editor published in the same issue of *Soldier:* "The Army will work for you if you work for the Army," he wrote. "Don't look for someone to give you something every time you do something ['right']. The Army is a job you can make work for you."

Indeed, many men and women have built enormously satisfying personal careers in military service while at the same time contributing to service-oriented missions and objectives. When they leave military service, these people are generally better human beings and conspicuously better citizens as a result of their training and experience. You can be among them if you can accept the challenges military service poses and work earnestly to meet them.

Implicit in any discussion of the "right stuff" are two factors of enormous importance to the military services: physical fitness and emotional stability. The demands of military service and the military life-style are such that both are receiving increasing emphasis by the Department of Defense in ways that could influence your eligibility for service.

The emphasis on physical fitness begins with the recruiting process and continues throughout any service career. Inability to meet the physical fitness requirements of the various services is probably the most important reason why recruits fail to complete basic training. Throughout your service career you will be under pressure to maintain a high standard of physical conditioning, including control of your body weight, no matter whether you are an infantryman or a desk-bound data processing specialist. The objective is not only to build muscles, but to achieve and maintain the enhanced well-being—physical, mental, and emotional—that accompanies good physical condition.

In this context, the Department of Defense has recently adopted a service-wide policy to reduce smoking and the use of tobacco products in the military services. Each service is responsible for its own antitobacco campaign, but the Army moved aggressively to ban smoking in all work areas and most public areas, effective July 1, 1986, and announced plans for smoking clinics and other antitobacco programs. The other services were expected to follow with similar measures. So, if you have begun smoking, you should give some serious thought to "kicking the habit."

In the category of emotional stability, the military services are placing even more emphasis on the problem of drug abuse. As has already been stated, use of illegal drugs can result in rejection of your application to enlist in any military service. Physical examinations include drug-screening tests. Prospective officers are subject to similar screening, of course. But that doesn't mean that you can resume (or start) using drugs once you have been accepted for service. During the years 1983 to 1985 the services discharged about 64,000 service men and women for drug abuse and disciplined an additional 79,000, according to a Department of Defense news release in July 1986. The campaign to eliminate drug abuse from the military services will obviously be accelerated in connection with the recently announced government-wide antidrug campaign. Once again, a word to the wise should be sufficient.

IS THERE A MILITARY LIFE-STYLE?

On the face of things, the answer to that question should be a resounding "Yes," if we take into account the well-defined service benefits and privileges and the persistence of ceremony, customs, and tradition throughout the services. On the other hand, many young men and women who enter military service these days find the flow of daily life little different from that of other work environments in small or mid-size civilian communities—once they have completed basic training, at least.

Elsewhere we have said that the military services are special communities. On the smaller scale, we could also say that the typical military installation resembles a small town. Each has most of the usual community and business services: offices, shops and stores, banks, restaurants, movie theaters, automobile service stations, schools, libraries, churches, social service agencies, youth programs, parks, and organized recreational facilities—along with its own police force, a legal staff (and courts), a fire department, a public utility department, and even a bus service. The installation head-quarters functions as "town hall."

One of the more obvious differences between a military installation and a civilian town is that most of the adults on the military installation wear uniforms while they work. And if some of these people whistle while they work, who can blame them?

The organization that employs them gives new members free board and room, furnishes their uniforms, and offers discount prices for food, clothing and other consumer items, and gasoline for their cars. While they are employed, they receive free medical and dental care; they can also purchase life insurance at rates well below market price. The same privileges are extended to military dependents. Service members receive thirty days' paid vacation each year. For those who qualify, there is the prospect of an attractive retirement package that includes all these benefits and more after service of as little as twenty years. Those who choose to leave the service before they are eligible for retirement may qualify for veterans' benefits under programs administered by the Veterans Administration and many of the states.

To a certain extent this kind of self-contained environment tends to isolate the military community from the civilian society in which it operates, though all military commands have public relations programs that include "outreach" to the civilian community. The fact remains, however, that civilians are excluded from using many military facilities even though most military installations in the United States are open to the public. Military police, however, control access to these installations; and the increasing concern about terrorist activity is leading to more stringent security measures in many instances.

Moreover, military personnel are not necessarily free to leave the installation at will. Peacetime "pass" and "leave" policies are liberal, especially in the United States, but unit and installation commanders may restrict or limit the movement of military members, usually in accordance with assigned missions. Disregarding these regulations can lead to disciplinary action, including possible imprisonment.

The military life is also characterized by periodic changes in assignment—usually routine, but not always—that require members to move to other locations and assume new duties. These moves can cause considerable disruption in individual lives. One solution is to "travel light" and not put down too many roots. For married personnel, however, that solution may not work at all.

Even without changes in permanent assignment, members of combat units may be sent on temporary duty to distant sites for training or manuevers; families are left behind. Naval personnel and Marines assigned to fleet operations may be at sea for months at a time. And there is always the prospect, however limited, that an emergency situation somewhere in the world will result in active fighting.

The military services recognize the problems that life in the service can cause, and they provide tax-exempt special allowances of various kinds that help meet individual needs. Included are allowances for housing and meals under some conditions, for uniforms (in some cases, for civilian clothing when the job assignment requires it), and for official travel (including changes in assignment from one place to another). Allowances are also paid to married personnel who serve in assignments that keep their families from joining them or to help with the extra expenses involved with assignments overseas. While these monetary considerations help smooth the way to some extent, life in the military requires a high degree of personal flexibility and a well-developed ability to cope with changing circumstances.

Some members of the military services are also entitled to extra, taxable "special pay." Special pay includes enlistment and reenlistment bonuses, hazardous duty pay (parachutists, bomb disposal experts, enlisted air crew members, for example), foreign duty and overseas incentive pay, "propay" (extra pay for achieving high levels of technical proficiency in certain jobs), sea duty pay, submarine duty pay, flight pay (for officers), diving pay, special pay for engineering and scientific officers (Air Force), and various supplements for medical officers.

On the brighter side, the military services also provide their members (and dependents) a wide variety of off-duty recreational facilities and programs. Clubs for junior enlisted members, non-commissioned officers, and commissioned officers often become centers for social activities at military installations. Other facilities and programs offer opportunities to participate in individual and organized sports, to engage in hobbies and handicrafts, to advance education, and to travel, usually at reduced rates.

In addition to activities supported by the military services, private nonprofit agencies such as the American Red Cross, the United Services Organization (USO), and various "emergency relief" agencies operate programs and facilities for service members and their families. National membership organizations like the Association of the United States Army and the Air Force Association work to improve the conditions of military service; in some ways, they may be thought of as lobbyists who represent the best interests of their military members in the corridors of Congress and the Pentagon.

LIFE IN THE FAST LANE

The single enlisted men and women who arrive at shore-based military installations in the United States after they complete basic training are usually assigned rooms in dormitories (once called "barracks") and take their meals in cafeteria-style dining halls. Dormitories and dining facilities vary from installation to installation and from service to service, but the emphasis in recent years has been on privacy and personal convenience. A fairly typical dormitory at a permanent military installation requires junior enlisted members to share rooms (two to a room is increasingly common) and to use common toilet and bath facilities. Unmarried senior enlisted men and women and officers usually have somewhat more elaborate living arrangements.

During the first year or so of your enlistment in any of the military services you can expect to be in a training or apprentice status. That is, you are kept busy mastering your skill field, learning the ropes, and improving your military proficiency. This is a critical period for recently enlisted men and women; they are watched closely for evidence of their ability to assume increased responsibility, their potential for leadership, and their suitability for long-term military service.

Job performance, along with on-the-job training, may be central to your daily routine. But you are also required to participate in a variety of purely military duties ranging from formal training classes to inspections, parades, and guard duty, depending upon the assignment and the installation. At times your days may be long and physically tiring, but personally satisfying. At other times you may be bored to death with inactivity.

Despite the work routine and the military requirements, you as a young male or female "single" may suddenly have an unusual amount of personal freedom compared to living at home with your parents or even rooming with other students at a college dormitory. How you use—or abuse—that freedom is perhaps one of the most difficult aspects of adjusting to life in military service. You are pretty much on your own, separated from family and friends. You probably do not have an automobile or other "wheels." And you have to make your own decisions about how to spend your free time.

All the military services encourage members to devote themselves to self-improvement during their off-duty time. Within the limitations of various duty stations, the services provide exceptional facilities for off-duty recreation. These usually include team and individual sports competitions, clubs and other hobby activities, opportunities for educational advancement, and travel and tour programs. You don't have to wonder what to do—just what to do first. And, if you are a little lonely, there are plenty of opportunities to make new friends with interests similar to yours.

Sports Programs and Other Recreational Services

The emphasis on physical conditioning common to the military services finds an outlet in off-duty facilities usually available to military personnel at little or no cost. Most bases and installations have gyms and physical fitness rooms, playing fields, tennis courts, bowling alleys, swimming pools, golf courses, and other athletic facilties.

Depending upon the installation and the geographic location, other popular sports activities include pistol and rifle marksmanship, skeet-shooting, running events, skiing, mountain climbing, "orienteering," backpacking, sport parachuting, white-water canoeing, horseback riding, sailing, and "volk marching." In most cases the necessary equipment (and, often, instruction) is provided or arranged by the installation.

Even the smallest military installations have competitive sports programs that start at the intramural level (usually at the unit of assignment) and extend to participation in interinstallation, service-wide, and interservice competition. The schedule for the 1986 Armed Forces Championships, for example, included as sports: powerlifting, marathon runs, boxing, wrestling, judo, volleyball, bowling, track and field events, raquetball, soccer, golf, softball, and tennis.

Those who are not interested in competing in sports may be interested in officiating at them. Coaching clinics are conducted at many installations to prepare coaches and other officials for the several levels of military sports competitions.

Members of the military services compete each year for positions on regional and national U.S. amateur athletic teams; some are good enough to be selected as members of the national teams that compete in the Olympic Games, the Pan American Games, and the Conseil Internationale du Sport Militaire, among others. One of the American contestants in the 1984 summer Olympic Games in Los Angeles, Second Lieutenant Alonzo C. Babers, was a 1983 graduate of the Air Force Academy. Babers won two gold medals in track events. He had previously run on U.S. track teams at the Pan American Games and the World University Games. He won gold medals in both competitions.

Other recreational facilities common to most military installations include picnic areas, campgrounds and RV parks, riding stables, and boating facilities. The facilities and services offered by one military service are usually available to members of all services. In some areas, usually outside the United States, joint-service recreational areas provide full-scale resort accommodations to military members and their families at rates scaled to the pay grade.

Hobbies and Handicrafts

Craft centers and hobby shops are part of the recreational facilities offered by most military installations; ceramics, woodworking, and

Second Lieutenant Alonzo C. Babers, U.S. Air Force Academy graduate, winner of two gold medals at the 1984 Olympic Games.

jewelry-making are examples. Some installations offer art classes, classes in dancing, courses in photography, and computer education, among other activities.

Many military installations have formed little theater groups that present plays to the public. Other special interest groups include chess clubs, stamp-collecting clubs, rod and reel clubs, personal computer clubs, and the like.

Educational Advancement

Members of the military services are offered exceptional opportunities for advancing their educational level during off-duty hours. Educational centers at most military installations provide free counseling, guidance, and testing for personnel. On-base programs range from preparation for the General Educational Development certificate (high school equivalency) to courses in English as a second language, to postgraduate courses offered by civilian universities. Excellent libraries are usually associated with these programs.

Participation in these programs is voluntary, but it may be worth noting that a high school diploma or equivalent is commonly required for promotion to non-commissioned officer grades; senior NCOs are expected to have at least an associate degree and preferably a bachelor's degree. Some tuition assistance is usually available to those in approved study programs.

Correspondence courses are available to both enlisted personnel and officers to help them improve job skills. A wide variety of courses is offered free of charge by technical institutes and advanced professional schools operated by the services themselves. Most services require completion of certain correspondence courses for promotion beyond the junior enlisted grades (E-2/E-3). Officers often obtain credit for attendance at advanced professional schools by means of correspondence courses and thus qualify for promotion.

Travel

Most military commands and installations operate full-scale travel services that offer economical group tours and individual travel arrangements comparable to those available from commercial travel agencies. Reduced fares are frequently offered by airline, bus, and rail companies to individuals (and often to military families) traveling on leave. In some cases, military members may travel on leave virtually free of charge by taking advantage of unused passenger space ("space available" travel) aboard military aircraft.

THE MILITARY FAMILY

The majority of military recruits and junior officers are unmarried when they enter active service, but even those who plan only brief careers in military service often marry while in uniform. Service marriages between active-duty members are becoming quite common, as well.

A rapid increase in the number of military families has been one of the more dramatic results of the decision to switch to all-volunteer military services. By the end of 1984 a little more than half of all enlisted men and women and about three fourths of all officers in the military establishment were married, representing more than a million spouses (wives and husbands) and a million and a half children.

These figures seem certain to increase each year as a result of policies that encourage junior enlisted men and women (E-1 to E-3) to marry. All barriers to eligibility for the Basic Allowance for Quarters, once awarded only to enlisted members at or above pay grade E-4, have been removed. This and other family allowances are now paid at grade E-1. The Air Force now accepts as recruits qualified married men and women who already have children. The Army has developed a program that offers married service couples the prospect for assignment together under certain conditions.

These developments are important because the two and a half million spouses and dependent children are directly or indirectly entitled to such benefits as health care, housing, education, the use of commissaries and base exchanges, travel expenses, and the expense of moving household goods and personal effects. While they may have been responsive to the needs of the general society, these developments have caused the military services unforeseen problems that in some cases have still to be sorted out and solved.

Thus, if you, as a teen-ager, are tempted to enlist when you graduate from high school, marry your childhood sweetheart after you complete basic training, and embark on a military career that some say offers "cradle to grave" care, hold on a bit!

The economic deck is stacked against you, despite the availability of family allowances, and probably won't improve until you have put in two or more years of service and are collecting the pay of an E-4, at least. Military housing is unlikely to be available to you, and rents for civilian housing near most military installations have skyrocketed. The cost of furnishing a new home can put you in debt for years. And, while your spouse may be willing to work to help make ends meet, job prospects at or around most military installations are not encouraging. Thousands of active-duty enlisted men and women who have married have suddenly found themselves existing at or below the official poverty level, hopelessly in debt, and dependent on food stamps and other forms of welfare.

More important, perhaps, is that the demands upon you during your first year or so of military service can cause intolerable strains to even the most solidly based marriage. That, in turn, can have adverse effects upon your job performance during a critical period of your military career. The divorce rate among young military couples is alarmingly high.

Not all the news is bad, of course. The well-being of the military family has become a high priority among military administrators. Many existing programs for military dependents have been expanded to meet urgent needs, and new ones are rapidly being established.

Centralized family support centers are more or less standard at major Army installations and are increasingly available at bases operated by the other services. They offer such services as orientation for new wives, temporary housing and the loan of essential household items, housing offices, employment counseling and job referral for spouses, and day-care centers for the children of two-income military families. Other counseling services are becoming common, and classes in cooking and nutrition, household budgeting and management, and prenatal and child care are more and more available. Military-oriented social service agencies usually operate in these family support centers; they include the Red Cross and the "emergency relief" associations.

The needs of the children of military families are receiving a great deal of attention. In addition to day-care centers for preschool children, military bases are now providing everything from supervised playgrounds to after-school programs that include organized sports (like the Little League), scouting programs, and teen clubs. Many off-duty military personnel are engaged in directing, supervising, and counseling participants in these programs.

WHEN JOHNNIE (OR JANE) COMES MARCHING HOME

The completion of any term of military service in peacetime is an event that should be preceded by thoughtful planning. The services provide the framework for converting young civilians into professional military personnel, but they generally leave them to cope with the problems involved in the transition back to civilian life. Depending upon your personal objectives, therefore, you should probably begin planning for your life after military service at about the same time that you are considering entering the service.

All the military services provide for generous pensions and other benefits after as little as twenty years of uniformed service, but comparatively few recruits stay long enough to enjoy them. Among other considerations, promotion policies for both enlisted and officer members consciously thin the ranks at the top of the military pyramid, and only the best-qualified are retained.

Thus, even if you join a military service with every intention of making a career, you may be weeded out along the way. And, if you aren't weeded out by the system, you may find that personal or family circumstances make it difficult or impossible to continue with your planned career of military service.

Unlike civilian employment, the longer you stay in military service, the more you may lose if you leave or are involuntarily separated before you are eligible for retirement. Under such circumstances, you may get nothing at all when you depart except, possibly, a lukewarm handshake and a figurative pat on the back. So, let's look a little more closely at what is involved and then explore some ways that may help make the system work for you.

Considerations for Returning to Civilian Society

The longer you remain on active duty in any military service, the more difficult it becomes to make the transition back to civilian life. This is true even for those who retire after twenty or more years of active service. A number of factors built into the military career system help to account for this situation.

To start with, the longer you remain in service, the more likely you are to take for granted benefits that are provided free or at low cost to military personnel but may be important items in a civilian budget: vocational and professional training; free room and board for single enlisted personnel and reduced rates for others; allowances for housing, food, and clothing; health care; low-cost life insurance; legal services; and assistance with preparing income tax returns, among other things.

Social and cultural reorientation also can accompany even a short term of military service, some simply a part of "growing up." You become independent of your parents, often at an early age. Military colleagues, often with widely varied backgrounds, replace former friends. You may decide to marry. Opportunities for advanced education and travel influence you more and more. You may have available clubs, restaurants, and other social and recreational facilities that cost considerably less than those in the civilian side of the economy. Along with growing up, you may find that your hometown no longer holds many attractions, but you haven't decided where you want to live when you leave the service.

Meanwhile, of course, the civilian world is changing, sometimes in subtle ways that you may not be aware of. Unless your military skill field has an exact civilian equivalent, you may find yourself competing against younger men and women with fewer technical qualifications and less experience, or with people of your own age and about the same work experience but with better educational qualifications. You may even find that you cannot find employment without some retraining. You may have to go back to school to catch up or to qualify for a new skill field.

These problems can usually be anticipated and measures taken to overcome them. For example:

1. Keep in touch with the civilian job market, especially if you are not planning to stay long in military service. Subscribe to publications in your field of interest, join professional or vocational societies, seek assistance from on-base counselors.

2. Find out what developments are occurring in your field; take advantage of the educational and training opportunities available while you are in uniform.

3. If you are in a confirmed career development program with long-term prospects, break the pattern and volunteer for an assignment that will put you into a civilian community for a tour of duty, perhaps as a recruiter or a Reserve instructor.

4. When you are close to the end of your term of service, attend one of the retirement planning seminars now becoming available; you do not have to be ready to retire to benefit from these seminars.

5. Use leave time to visit areas where you think you may want to settle down. Get as much information as possible in advance, from the Chamber of Commerce and the local newspaper, and take along your family if you have one. Have your spouse check out schools, churches, housing, recreational facilities, and other community assets while you contact potential employers.

Of course, none of these steps will help you very much unless you have worked out a financial plan that will enable you to sail through some of the predictable obstacles to your return to civilian society. The sooner you do this, the better off you are, especially if you are considering making a career of military service. In a few words, that means living within your income, avoiding "impulse" purchase of luxury items, and contributing regularly to a savings program.

Military Retirement

Retirement with pay after a career of military service can, of course, pose fewer reentry problems than if you leave the service sooner, but sound planning is still essential.

Legislation passed by the United States Congress in mid-1986 revised the long-standing retirement scheme for the military services effective August 1, 1986. The thrust of the new legislation is to penalize those who retire with less than thirty years of service, though the penalty is small and its effects are canceled out when the retiree reaches age 62. Military members on active duty prior to August 1, 1986, members retiring with disabilities incurred during active service, survivors, and reservists are not affected by the new law, known as P.L. 99–348.

The new system retains the "multiplier" of 2.5 percent of base pay for each year of satisfactory service, but it imposes a penalty of 1 percent for each year an active-duty member retires before reaching thirty years of service. In addition, base pay is calculated from the so-called High-3; that is, base pay for retirement purposes is the average of the last three years of actual base pay, not the base pay you might have earned during your final year in service.

Thus, a military member who enters on active duty after August 1,

1986, and who retires with twenty years' service will be entitled to retirement pay based on forty percent of his or her High-3 pay. The figure is arrived at as follows:

Years of Service (YOS): 20
Multiplier per year: 2.5%
Retirement Entitlement: 20 × 2.5% = 50% of High-3
YOS Penalty (YOS less than 30): 10%
Actual Retirement Pay: 40% of High-3

Retirement with more than twenty years but less than thirty years of service would, of course, reduce the penalty. For example, retirement with twenty-four years of service would result in a pension based on 54 percent of High-3; the penalty now would only be 6 percent.

The penalty is entirely removed when you have served for thirty years. Thus, your immediate retirement pay would then be 75 percent of High-3, the same as before enactment of P.L. 99–348. And, in any event, the penalty is removed at age 62 for those who were initially penalized because they had not served on active duty for thirty years. That is, based on the two examples above, the person who retires with only twenty years of service will receive an adjusted retirement pay based on 50 percent of the High-3 beginning at age 62; the one who retires with 54 percent of High-3 for twenty-four years of service will receive the full 60 percent of his or her High-3 at age 62.

The law also provides for an annual cost-of-living allowance based on the Consumer Price Index minus one percent; this is known as CPI-1. However, at age 62 another adjustment occurs. At that time, the retirement pay is recalculated as though the cost-of-living allowance had been equal to the Consumer Price Index for every year after retirement. This adjustment will result in a considerable increase in retirement pay at age 62 for everyone, but particularly for those who retired with less than thirty years of service.

You should also remember that you make no contributions toward your final retirement pension, though you do contribute to the general Social Security retirement fund throughout your service. The increased pension at age 62 under the terms of P.L. 99–348, incidentally, coincides with the earliest year in which you may become eligible for a Social Security pension—at least, as of this writing. The net effect will be to entitle you to a rather significant pension at age 62 if you choose to accept the Social Security pension.

Military retirees and eligible dependents are also entitled to most of the benefits they received while they were on active duty: free or low-cost health care, use of military commissaries and exchanges, legal services, and use of such military facilities as movie theaters, hobby shops, travel and tours, and other recreational facilities. Largely for this reason, incidentally, many military retirees settle in states or communities close to military bases.

California, Texas, Florida, and Virginia had the largest populations of military retirees in 1985. Those four states, along with Georgia, Washington, North Carolina, Pennsylvania, South Carolina, and New York were home to about fifty-five percent of all military retirees in that year. State tax rules may also influence decisions about where to retire; among the states listed, Texas and Florida had no state income taxes; Pennsylvania did not tax pension income.

All this appears to add up to quite a generous pension until you understand that the actual pension income is some percentage of your *base pay* and not of your final month's earnings—which may include housing allowance, subsistence allowances, uniform allowance, special pay, or other supplemental income. Retirement planners generally recommend that family income should be about eighty percent of preretirement earnings to maintain the same standard of living. In most cases, therefore, military retirement with fewer than thirty years of service almost always means that the "retired" member must build a second career. Thirty years' service assures a better pension and a more solid economic base, but job prospects are likely to be more restricted.

Sound planning can help make a comfortable transition from military to civilian life, of course. Savings, investments, and the purchase of a home during active service can ease the financial burden; such home purchases are possible under a program administered by the Veterans Administration. The importance of taking advantage of advanced technical training and education while still in service is obvious. Second-career employment counseling and placement services are offered by the Veterans Administration, most state offices of veterans' affairs, and organizations such as the Retired Officers Association and the Retired Non-Commissioned Officers Association. A useful handbook for those interested in further details is the *Retired Military Almanac*, published annually by Uniformed Services Almanac, Inc., PO Box 76, Washington, DC 20004.

Benefits of Short Term Military Service.

Those who serve in the military services for a limited time, whether by design or circumstance, may still benefit materially, although they will not have acquired any pension rights except with respect to the Social Security contributions they have made while in service. Honorably discharged veterans are, of course, entitled to certain benefits under the Veterans Administration programs discussed below. With proper planning and a great deal of energy, it is possible to acquire a highly marketable skill or trade during only one enlistment. Meanwhile, most of the other advantages of military service, particularly opportunities for educational advancement, are available to enlisted members and officers who do not aspire to military careers.

A few words of caution may be in order. If you wish to explore training in a high-tech area, for example, be certain that you understand all the strings attached to the enlisted or officer programs offered by the various services. The best training programs are not always available to those who select short terms of enlistment, for instance. Shorter periods of active duty also result in longer obligations to serve in a Reserve status. Some technical training programs may carry an obligation to serve beyond the initial period of active duty. In general, of course, the longer you remain on active duty— short of qualifying for retirement—the more difficult it becomes to make a smooth transition back to civilian life.

In addition to the opportunities for self-improvement offered in active military service, honorably discharged veterans are eligible for a variety of benefits administered by the Veterans Administration, and many may qualify for benefits available from their home state.

Recently discharged enlisted men and women may also utilize their military experience to gain an officer's commission in a college-sponsored Reserve Officers Training Corps (ROTC) program. They receive credit for prior military training that helps to shorten the training requirement; and they receive a monthly allowance during the two years of advanced ROTC training. Others may be able to supplement their income as citizen soldiers by participating in Selected Reserve training.

Veterans' Benefits

The Veterans Administration (VA) offers a number of postservice benefits to honorably discharged military veterans. Many states also have programs for veterans who are residents; the programs vary widely, and information about them is best obtained directly from the state or from your educational center while you are in active service.

One of the most important of the federal programs, and among the newest, is the Veteran's Educational Assistance Program, known as "the new GI Bill." The program is designed to provide postservice educational opportunities, including educational and vocational counseling. However, the program requires participation by the service member while he or she is on active duty.

Eligible enlisted military personnel may contribute up to one hundred dollars a month for up to thirty-six months to an educational fund established in their name. The government contributes an amount double that of the individual contribution. When the enlisted member leaves the service or retires, he or she may receive up to three hundred dollars a month in educational assistance while attending an approved college or university, junior college, or other educational institution.

Other programs administered by the VA include vocational rehabilitation for veterans with service-connected physical disabilities, readjustment counseling, and the "old" GI Bill, eligibility for which expires December 31, 1989.

Veterans who have become disabled during active military service may also benefit from pensions, free medical service, dental treatment, vocational rehabilitation, and low-cost life insurance.

An important function of the VA is that of providing health care for veterans. Eligibility for treatment at VA hospitals and clinics varies from time to time but is usually conditional upon the existence of a service-connected disability or the inability of the veteran to pay for treatment in a civilian hospital.

In yet another area, the VA guarantees loans made by veterans for the purchases of houses, condominiums, and manufactured homes. As noted above, this program is available to military personnel on active duty and not limited to discharged veterans.

Other programs exist that have not been mentioned here. Further information may be found in the annual VA publication *Federal Benefits for Veterans and Dependents*, available from the Superintendent of Documents, U.S. Government Printing Office, Washington, DC 20402.

Chapter **XI**

You and the Reserve Forces

As we began our exploration of military careers with a look at the traditional American institution of the citizen soldier, it seems important to end with a closer examination of how that still important institution works today.

The modern reserve forces of the military services are, in effect, mirror images of their active-duty sponsors. Many young men and women have been able to carve out rewarding careers in the reserves as an alternative to full-time military service. They are the true citizen soldiers, with firm roots in their community, honoring a well-established American tradition. But they train and operate in an environment that can keep them in close contact with the active forces, entitle them to technical training and educational benefits that match—and, in some cases, exceed—those available to their active-duty counterparts, and eventually even qualify them for military retirement with a pension and all the benefits and privileges enjoyed by career military retirees.

Several alternatives for service in the reserves are available to qualified men and women, and we shall be concerned with three of them:

1. Noncareer service in the reserves that can satisfy short-term personal objectives. You might think of this as a bridge to a civilian career, since reserve service can give you technical training for a civilian job and opportunities for college scholarships and even postgraduate professional studies—and pay you while you study.

2. Service in the reserves after completion of some period of active military service, enlisted or commissioned, as a "cooling off" device while you make the transition from military to civilian status. You can make valuable contacts and earn money for a while as you become adjusted to your new role. You can also, of course, continue to enjoy many of the benefits of active military service and even qualify for additional educational benefits.

Many former active service NCOs and officers who have left active service with a substantial number of years to their credit join the active reserves to acquire enough time to retire under one of the reserve retirement programs.

3. Career service in the reserves, without prior active-duty training or experience, as an attractive, often prestigious alternative to a full-time military career. You can acquire technical training and advanced education, secure a commission as an officer if you are interested, and even qualify for military retirement after twenty years of federal service. You can enjoy many of the benefits of military service while you are in the reserves without interference with your civilian occupational or professional goals; indeed, career service in the reserves may offer opportunities to enhance your qualifications in a civilian career field.

Before we explore these alternatives, however, you should know a bit more about how the reserves are organized and how they fit into the total defense establishment of the United States.

THE ROLE OF THE RESERVES IN THE TOTAL FORCE

During the past decade or so, all five military services of the United States have adopted a concept that influences every aspect of the defense establishment. The concept is that of the "total force" and means that each military service includes in its peacetime organization a "reserve" component that can be counted on as part of that service if needed under emergency conditions.

To put the concept into practice, each service has had to place additional emphasis on the development of a reserve force organized, equipped, and trained just like the active force. Thus, the distinctions that once set the "reserves" apart are being done away with. Those in the reserves wear the same uniforms, hold the same ranks, train in the same military occupational specialties alongside their active service counterparts, and enjoy all the benefits and privileges afforded the "regular" forces.

The reserves have already become an important factor in the overall planning for the defense of the United States and its interests. Reservists serve on active duty with the regular forces; many reserve units and individual reservists participate in the annual maneuvers and training exercises staged each year by the regular forces in the United States and elsewhere around the world. Other reserve units perform operational tasks that support the active services and keep the units and their members at a high state of readiness.

One way to clarify the still-growing importance of the reserves is by numbers. In 1985 the reserve components of the five military services included about 1.5 million men and women. Projections for 1990 envisage a reserve force of about 2.1 million members, about the same as the number in the active forces. The National Guard and the five service Reserves make up the reserve force.

The National Guard organization is the direct descendant of the state militias of our earlier national history and may even be compared to the colonial militias established under British rule. There are fifty-four National Guard organizations, one for each state and one each in the District of Columbia, Puerto Rico, the Virgin Islands, and Guam, Each state or territorial Guard is under the control of the governor, who has the authority to appoint officers, establish training facilities, and call on Guardsmen for assistance in the event of natural disaster or civil disorder. However, these state organizations may be "federalized" in time of national emergency and assigned missions as part of the national military forces.

The National Guard was originally a ground force, but the establishment of the Air Force led to its division into the Army National Guard and the Air National Guard. The Army National Guard is the largest combat-ready element of the Army's reserve force, and many combat units have been assigned missions that augment the active Army forces. The Air Force relies less upon the Air National Guard for direct combat augmentation; instead, it has assigned the Guard many supporting or auxiliary missions, including the development and training of the aviation units largely responsible for the defense of the continental United States.

The reserve components of the military services provide the balance of the reserve manpower. They are usually designated as the service reserve: U.S. Army Reserve, U.S. Marine Corps Reserve, and so on. They are controlled directly by the parent services, though policies and guidelines developed by the Department of Defense make them similar in many respects. For example, each service Reserve includes the following categories:

• Selected Reserve, made up of the highly trained units and individuals most likely to be called to active duty ("mobilized") in time of emergency. Those assigned to Selected Reserve units are usually paid to attend regular monthly drill periods and perform two weeks of active duty for training purposes each year. Individuals in this category may be assigned duties under mobilization plans; they usually serve two-week tours of training duty each year.

• Individual Ready Reserve, a pool of skilled (pretrained) people not assigned to mobilization units but subject to recall to active service as individual replacements. This category includes most of the men and women who still have reserve obligations when they leave active military service (after a single enlistment or at the completion of a reserve officer's obligated tour, for example). The majority of people in this category do not participate in any organized training.

• Standby Reserve, a small group of people who have completed their statutory six-year reserve obligation and are unassigned to any mobilization mission; they are subject to mobilization only in case of national emergency.

The majority of those in the reserve force at this time are designated as part of the Army reserve force. The Army National Guard and the Army Reserve between them account for about one million men and women. This figure reflects the fact that nearly half the wartime mission of the Army is assigned to its reserve forces. The table below provides comparable data for all the armed services as of 1985.

While the organization of the reserve components follows that of the parent organization, that does not mean that the reserve component is a carbon copy of the active service. In most cases the composition of the reserve component reflects the assignment of particular mobilization or wartime missions. The Army National Guard has as its primary mission the defense of the continental United States and its territories. The Army Guard is heavy in the combat arms and combat support areas: infantry, armor, artillery, engineers, aviation (helicopters), military police, and communications, for example. By way of comparison, Army Reserve units tend to emphasize medical units, civil affairs and military government, psychological operations, logistical support commands, and transportation services; there are, of course, some combat arms and combat support units in the Army Reserve, as well.

The Air National Guard and the Air Force Reserve show similar variations in composition. The Air Guard contribution in aviation specialties tends to emphasize interceptors, tactical fighter-bombers, tactical airlift, and tactical air control. Air Force Reserve units and

RESERVE FORCE CONTRIBUTION TO THE "TOTAL FORCE"

Military Service and Reserve Strength	Active Forces	National Guard	Reserves
Army (1,006,342)	52%	30%	18%
Navy (194,551)	82%	—	18%
Marine Corps (85,941)	84%	—	16%
Air Force (218,760)	76%	14%	10%
Coast Guard (15,000)*	73%	—	17%

* Figures for Coast Guard are estimates.

flight officers are more likely to be involved with weather reconnaissance, strategic airlift, cargo and tanker operations, aeromedical
evacuation, and logistical support to the Air Force. The Air Force
uses its reserves for operational support: Air Force Reserve units
flew nearly 100,000 passengers, medically evacuated about 80,000
patients, and air-dropped some 37 airborne units during fiscal year
1984. During the same year, Air Force Reserve pilots flew seventy
percent of the hurricane reconnaissance missions over the Gulf of
Mexico and flew more than 82,000 hours in C-141s and C-5s, mostly
in logistical support of the active Air Force.

The Navy's reserve forces are largely dedicated to the performance
of missions in a general war; logistical airlift, military sealift, cargo
loading, shipping control, and minesweeping are all missions assigned
primarily to the Naval Reserve. The Naval Reserve is also heavy on
combat engineering (the Seabees) and special boat forces, though not
on surface combatant ships. More emphasis in the combat area is
given to naval air units than to surface ships, though this situation
may change.

As you might expect, the Marine Corps Reserve is pretty much the
exception. A large majority of the reserve force is oriented around
the Fourth Marine Division, essentially a carbon copy of the other
three that make up the Fleet Marine Force. Except for civil affairs,
entirely assigned to the Reserve, and Force Reconnaissance, the
Marine Corps Reserve consists largely of combat arms and combat
support units suited largely to augmentation.

SERVICE IN THE RESERVE FORCES

Entering the reserve forces is very much like entering the active
forces, though enlistments are generally for six years. Enlisted
recruits with no prior military training are usually ordered to active
duty for about six months to complete basic training and attend
technical school. In most cases, recruits can split the active-duty time
into two periods, taking basic training during the first summer and
technical training during the second. Recruits are paid at the regular
rate for their grade during active-duty periods.

Those with some active military training and experience usually are
able to join a Selected Reserve unit in the same grade and with the
same military occupational specialty that they had during their active-
duty service. In some cases, it may be possible to join a Selected
Reserve unit and be retrained in another MOS.

In either case, once you join a Selected Reserve unit, you are
required to attend drill two days a month, almost always on week-

ends, and a two-week training session each year. You are paid for four days when you attend each two-day weekend drill; during the two-week training session, you receive the pay and allowances for your grade and years of service.

Once you have enlisted in the Reserves, you are eligible for all the benefits and privileges of regular military service at appropriate times and places. For example, Reservists have limited access to exchange facilities and can use military commissaries only during their annual periods of active duty. They are entitled to medical treatment only while on active duty for training purposes.

What seems more important at this point, however, is that service with the Reserves can qualify you for appointment to a service academy or enable you to apply for an ROTC scholarship; either route can be used to earn a commission as an officer while you are getting what is essentially a free college education.

When you have completed college, you may be able to obtain additional financial assistance through the military service to enable you to attend law school or medical school. You may have to spend additional time on active duty when you obtain your professional degree, but you don't have to make the service a career.

If you don't win an ROTC scholarship, however, you might be interested in an Army program that enables you to participate in an Army Reserve unit while you are attending college and enrolled in the ROTC program. You can be paid for both activities. This is a particuarly attractive option for young men and women who have already served a tour of duty with the active forces: you are given credit for your earlier military training and experience and excused from the first two years of ROTC training. In fact, you may be commissioned at the end of your sophomore year in college and thus be entitled to higher pay for your Army Reserve service. Promotions through the officer ranks to general officer grades are possible, if you want to stay the course.

In the event that a college education is not your goal, you can still benefit from the technical training that you receive, especially if you can turn the training and subsequent military experience into a civilian job. While you are in the reserve unit, of course, you can also anticipate advanced technical training that may enhance your civilian job performance; you can also benefit from the correspondence courses provided by most of the services.

Just as in the active service, you can expect promotions as you gain skills and experience. With promotions come increases in pay and prestige. As time goes on you may move into supervisory positions, along with opportunities to attend courses in leadership and management—giving you, perhaps, another boost to your civilian job qualifications. The enlisted career ladder in the reserves runs right through to the top, of course.

Meanwhile, you are developing roots in your own community and not subject to many of the problems that members of the regular military forces face from time to time. Most employers recognize the importance of the reserve and cooperate by giving their employees time off for training activities, especially during the two-week annual period, without charging them for vacation time. As you serve with the reserve forces you are acquiring credits toward a military retirement that can give you additional income and security in later years.

Every military service has its own programs and inducements to make service in their reserve forces more attractive. Space does not permit us to mention them all. The Army Reserve, for example, offers a choice of an enlistment bonus of two thousand dollars or educational assistance of four thousand dollars, spread over four years, just for joining. Reserve service also may help you reduce a student loan you have taken out for college expenses: For every year you serve in the reserves, you may receive credit for "repayment" of fifteen percent of your loan or five hundred dollars, whichever is greater.

The recruiting offices of the military services have a great deal of information about the reserves; and the local reserve units in or near your community have active recruiting programs. If you are interested, you should talk with these people.

MILITARY RETIREMENT IN THE RESERVES

Reservists who serve for twenty "creditable" years are eligible for pensions and all the retirement benefits enjoyed by those who retire from the active forces. The basis for calculating retirement credits is different from that of the active services, however; and you cannot collect any pension until the age of sixty. This may seem like a long way off, but you should at least have an idea how the system works. In addition, as noted above, the reserve retirement can be an important alternative to regular military retirement for men and women who joined a service with career intentions but were unable to serve the minimum twenty years.

Retirement from the reserve components is based on a point system that is the same for both enlisted members and officers. Points are awarded for service of various kinds, starting with one point for each day of active duty. Other points are awarded for armory drills:

four points may be earned for each two-day weekend drill, for example. Points are also awarded for completion of military correspondence courses, for time spent in preparing military instruction, and for time spent on unit administration. Retention in active reserve status requires accumulating at least fifty points during each twelve-month period. But, happily, just being in active reserve status automatically awards fifteen points each year.

Under this system, members of Selected Reserve units who attend twelve weekend drills and the two-week annual training period are awarded a minimum of seventy-seven points. Those who have mobilization assignments receive points for their annual two-week active-duty tour; but they may also be able to earn additional points as members of non-pay composite reserve units and by attending reserve schools or taking correspondence courses, among other things.

As you continue service in the reserves, points build up year by year. A minimum of twenty "creditable" years is required for retirement, and your Reserve Personnel Center will notify you when you arrive at that point. But how do you know what kind of pension to expect?

At the time you retire, you simply total all the points you have accumulated and divide by 360. The result is a figurative number of "years of service." You next multiply years of service by 2.5 percent to arrive at the percent of your base pay that you will receive as pension. Of course, the more points you have accumulated, the larger your pension will be. That is why it is very worthwhile for those who have several, or many, years of active duty behind them to join the reserves and stay until they have their twenty years.

Complicated? An example may help, but we cannot give you a dollar figure; that will be calculated only when you approach age sixty, and by then the pay tables will have changed.

Let's assume that you have reached the twenty-year mark as an Army Major, after having turned an enlistment in the Army Reserve into a commission by way of ROTC and serving five years on active duty. You have accumulated 3,600 points for reserve service. Here is what you do:

1. Divide 3,600 points by 360 to obtain years of service: the result is 10 years.
2. Multiply 10 years by .025 to obtain percent of pay due: the result is .250, or twenty-five percent of base pay.
3. Consult pay table to determine monthly pension amount: using 1987 pay table, your pension is $705.00 per month.

However, you are only thirty-nine years old now; you won't begin to receive your pension until you are sixty years of age, twenty-one years from now. By that time, you may have been promoted again and then decided to "retire," at age fifty. You still have to wait ten years, but that reserve pension is like having money in the bank, lots of money in the bank. And every time Congress increases military pay, you have more, in effect.

Meanwhile as a member of the Retired Reserve you have some military benefits. At age sixty, you will be entitled to all of them. This seems a very sensible thing to do. Even though your sixtieth birthday may be a long way in the future, you will have earned the gratitude of your fellow citizens for your participation in the reserves, you will have gained personally in many ways, and you will have a certain satisfaction in having performed a service for your country. And that, when it comes down to it, is what it means to be a citizen soldier.

APPENDICES

Enlisted Pay and Allowances

APPENDIX A.   ENLISTED PAY AND ALLOWANCES

1. REPRESENTATIVE BASE PAY (ANNUAL FIGURES)

Pay Grade	Years of Service									
	Under 2	2	3	4	6	8	10	20	26	
E-9	*	*	*	*	*	*	$23,688	$26,410	$30,503	E-9
E-8	*	*	*	*	*	$19,868	20,434	23,148	27,241	E-8
E-7	*	*	*	*	$16,621	17,270	17,698	20,426	24,509	E-7
E-6	$11,934	$13,007	$13,550	$14,126	$14,652	$15,185	15,743	17,892	17,892	E-6
E-5	10,472	11,401	11,952	12,474	13,291	13,831	14,382	15,185	15,185	E-5
E-4	9,770	10,314	10,919	11,768	12,233	*	*	*	*	E-4
E-3	9,202	9,706	10,098	10,498	*	*	*	*	*	E-3
E-2	8,856	*	*	*	*	*	*	*	*	E-2
E-1	7,898#	*	*	*	*	*	*	*	*	E-1

NOTES:
* Enlisted personnel with these years of service are not likely to be in this grade.
# Pay for E-1's with less than four month's service (Recruits) is $608.40 per month.
Source: Department of Defense (Pay Tables effective 1/1/87)

2. BASIC ALLOWANCE FOR QUARTERS, PER MONTH (BAQ)

	E-1	E-2	E-3	E-4	E-5	E-6	E-7	E-8	E-9
Without Dependents	$141.60	$155.40	$183.00	$188.40	$217.20	$234.90	$264.60	$309.90	$334.50
With Dependents	253.20	253.20	253.20	275.40	318.60	358.50	395.10	424.80	456.00

3. BASIC ALLOWANCE FOR SUBSISTENCE, PER DAY (BAS)

	E-1 (under 4 mos)	All Others
When rations in kind are not available	$5.61	$6.07
When on leave or permission to mess separately	4.96	5.37
When no Government mess available (Emergency)	7.43	8.03

Appendix **B**

Officer Pay and Allowances

APPENDIX B. OFFICER PAY AND ALLOWANCES

1. REPRESENTATIVE BASE PAY (ANNUAL FIGURES)

a. Commissioned Officers

Pay Grade	Under 2	2	3	4	6	8	10	20	26
					Years of Service				
O-10	*	*	*	*	*	*	*	$70,801	$70,801
O-9	*	*	*	*	*	*	*	70,801	70,801
O-8	*	*	*	*	*	*	*	68,372	70,801
O-7	*	*	*	*	*	*	*	62,734	62,734
O-6	*	*	*	*	*	*	$37,350	48,035	55,120
O-5	*	*	*	*	$32,036	$32,036	33,008	43,456	44,971
O-4	*	$26,194	$27,940	$27,940	28,458	29,714	31,741	37,607	37,607
O-3	$19,991	22,349	23,986	26,435	27,698	28,696	30,247	32,522	32,522
O-2	17,426	19,037	22,867	22,867	23,638	24,134	24,134	24,134	24,134
O-1	15,131	15,754	19,037	19,037	19,037	19,037	19,037	19,037	19,037

b. Warrant Officers

Pay Grade	Under 2	2	3	4	6	8	10	20	26
W-4	*	*	$21,848	$23,349	$23,334	$24,394	$25,420	$31,223	$34,780
W-3	*	$20,077	20,077	20,336	20,574	22,078	23,364	27,461	29,455
W-2	$16,211	17,539	17,539	18,050	19,037	20,077	20,840	24,646	25,639
W-1	13,507	15,487	15,487	16,780	17,539	18,292	19,037	22,867	22,867

* NOTE: Personnel with this service would not usually be in the grade indicated.
Source: DOD Pay Tables, 1/1/87.

2. BASIC ALLOWANCE FOR QUARTERS, PER MONTH (BAQ)

	O-1	O-2	O-3	O-4	O-5	O-6	O-7	O-8	O-9	O-10
Without Dependents	$253.20	$295.20	$366.60	$452.70	$493.80	$523.20	$570.00	$570.00	$570.00	$570.00
With Dependents	343.20	382.80	446.40	535.50	585.90	636.00	701.10	701.10	701.00	701.10

3. BASIC ALLOWANCE FOR SUBSISTENCE, PER MONTH (BAS)
For all Officers, Warrant Officers, Aviation Cadets: $112.65

Enlisted Military Occupations

The 134 Military Occupations listed here have been extracted from the 1985 edition of *Military Career Guide*, published by the Department of Defense. Each of the Military Occupations describes a career field that includes one or more specializations; altogether, more than 2,000 occupational specialties may be found within the five military services. Once a Military Occupation has been selected for preliminary career planning, a recruiter for the service of choice should be consulted about the availability of specific specializations. The user may also refer to the table in Chapter III for information concerning equivalent or related civilian career options.

The following notes on the arrangement of the information should be helpful to the user:

1. Column 1 lists the Military Occupations in alphabetical order, rather than by the twelve broad career fields that are listed in Chapter III.

2. Column 2 shows which military services offer any given Military Occupation. The symbol (A) under a service heading indicates that the Department of Labor (DOL) has accepted military schooling and on-the-job training as equal to an apprenticeship program in one or more of the specializations within that Military Occupation. Upon satisfactory completion of the apprenticeship, DOL awards the

ENLISTED MILITARY OCCUPATIONAL FIELDS

Column 1 *Military Occupation*	*Column 2* *Services Offering Occupation*				
	ARMY	USAF	USCG	NAVY	MARINES
Accounting Specialists	x	x	x	x	x
Administrative Support Specialists	x	x	x	x	x
Air Crew Members (#)	x	x	x	x	x
Air Traffic Controllers	x	x	x	x	x
Aircraft Electricians	(A)	x	x	(A)	(A)

person a certificate of journeyman status that is recognized by industrial and trade unions and civilian employers.

3. Column 3 gives the estimated number of jobs in each Military Occupation existing in all five military services as of 1985. No major changes are anticipated.

4. Column 4 estimates the number of replacement workers needed each year.

5. Column 5 shows, by ASVAB occupational group, the test scores a prospective recruit must have to be reasonably sure of being qualified for a particular Military Occupation. Test scores are given as a range, showing the 90 and 95 percentiles of the youth population. Because entry-level scores may vary from service to service, and from time to time, this information is only for planning purposes. Moreover, a high ASVAB occupational score may not, of itself, qualify the candidate for entry into any Military Occupation; other ASVAB scores are also taken into consideration.

ASVAB occupational scores are approximated, and the occupational fields appear in abbreviated form:

M&C = Mechanical and Crafts
B&C = Business and Clerical
E&E = Electronic and Electrical
HS&T = Health, Social, and Technology

6. The duration of entry-level training is shown in Column 6 as a range of weeks. In most cases, training includes classroom instruction and shop or laboratory sessions, as appropriate; in some cases, field exercises are also included. The range of weeks given indicates that training varies according to the specialties included in a given Military Occupation.

7. In Column 7 are, as available, Department of Labor estimates of percentage growth in the number of equivalent or related civilian jobs through the year 1995. Growth rates in the order of 20-27 percent over the period are considered average.

Column 3 No. of Jobs	Column 4 Annual Rqmnt.	Column 5 ASVAB Scores		Column 6 Training (Weeks)	Column 7 DOL %
10,100	1,010	B&C	53–61	8–12	16–40%
75,600	10,600	B&C	47–55	7–10	16%
3,500	360	HS&T	47–55	7– 9	
11,800	1,230	HS&T	37–48	7–13	4%
11,100	1,320	E&E	43–50	18–25	32%

Military Occupation	ARMY	USAF	USCG	NAVY	MARINES
Aircraft Launch and Recovery Specialists (#)				x	x
Aircraft Mechanics	(A)	x	x	x	x
Artillery Crew Members (#)	x		x	x	x
Audiovisual Production Specialists	(A)	x	x	(A)	x
Automobile Mechanics	(A)	x	x	x	(A)
Automotive Body Repairers	(A)	x		x	x
Barbers			x	x	
Blasting Specialists	(A)	x		x	x
Boat Operators	x	x	x	x	
Boiler Technicians			x	(A)	
Bricklayers and Concrete Masons	(A)	x		x	x
Broadcast and Recording Technicians	(A)	x		x	x
Building Electricians	(A)	x	x	x	(A)
Cardiopulmonary and EEG Specialists	x	x		x	
Cargo Specialists	x	x	x	x	x
Carpenters	(A)	x	x	x	x
Caseworkers and Counselors	x	x	x	x	x
Clothing and Fabric Repairers	x	x		x	x
Combat Engineers	x	x	x	x	x
Compressed Gas Technicians	x	x		x	x
Computer Operators	x	x	x	x	x
Computer Programmers	x	x	x	x	x
Computer Systems Analysts	x	x		x	x
Construction Equipment Operators	(A)	x		x	x
Corrections Specialists	x			x	x
Court Reporters	x	x	x	x	x
Data Entry Specialists	x	x	x	x	x
Data Processing Equipment Repairers	(A)	x		x	(A)
Dental Laboratory Technicians	x	x	x	x	
Dental Specialists	x	x	x	x	
Detectives	x	x	x	x	x
Dispatchers	x	x		x	x
Divers	x		x	x	x
Drafters (Construction)	(A)	x	x	x	x
Electrical Products Repairers	(A)	x	x	(A)	(A)
Electronic Instrument Repairers	(A)	x		x	x
Electronic Weapons Systems Repairers	(A)	x	x	(A)	(A)
Emergency Management Specialists	x	x	x	x	x
Engine Mechanics	(A)	x	x	(A)	(A)
Environmental Health Specialists	x	x	x	x	x
Firefighters	(A)	x	x	x	x
Flight Engineers		x		x	x
Flight Operations Specialists	x	x	x	x	x

No. of Jobs	Annual Rqmnt.	ASVAB Scores		Training (Weeks)	DOL %
3,150	830	M&C	55–70	9–13	
142,000	16,100	M&C	45–55	3–17	19%
64,900	14,100	HS&T	30–37	10–14	
1,540	160	HS&T	38–49	7–12	27%
41,000	8,300	M&C	41–46	8–12	38%
2,430	250	M&C	38–46	11–15	40%
640	65	HS&T	47–55	4– 6	10%
500	90	M&C	44–51	6–10	
1,850	190	M&C	48–56	16–22	
4,670	500	M&C	56–65	12–16	
5,100	840	M&C	39–46	5– 8	33%
780	80	HS&T	38–48	9–52	27%
1,870	300	E&E	39–46	8–12	32%
560	80	HS&T	37–47	26–30	37%
6,200	1,030	M&C	34–45	2– 6	18%
5,900	1,050	M&C	39–47	6– 8	29%
2,870	190	HS&T	53–65	8–10	21%
3,290	400	M&C	32–40	6– 8	
18,800	3,610	HS&T	37–45	USMC–6/OJT	
1,640	170	M&C	47–55	14–19	
10,900	1,640	HS&T	38–45	7–12	27%
3,150	480	HS&T	46–55	10–13	77%
2,110	220	HS&T	46–58	10–18	85%
9,500	1,820	M&C	34–43	8– 9	44%
2,850	360	HS&T	32–40	5–10	33%
600	60	B&C	57–67	6–10	
3,630	410	B&C	42–50	8–13	27%
8,200	820	E&E	64–70	25–35	61%
2,200	220	HS&T	42–52	22–24	26%
7,200	1,100	HS&T	36–40	9–14	42%
1,890	190	HS&T	49–57	10–12	8%
6,000	870	M&C	42–50	7–17	
3,100	600	M&C	54–65	5–13	
970	170	HS&T	39–48	10–11	5%
8,560	860	E&E	41–47	4–24	61%
17,100	1,980	E&E	61–66	15–30	61%
23,000	3,120	E&E	41–50	15–30	
2,320	120	HS&T	62–78	8–10	
20,000	3,060	M&E	40–50	7–23	
3,630	520	HS&T	38–48	11–19	
12,100	1,470	HS&T	30–36	7–11	9%
2,820	290	E&E	68–75	17–24	
5,700	570	HS&T	42–50	7–14	

Military Occupation	ARMY	USAF	USCG	NAVY	MARINES
Food Service Specialists	(A)	x	x	(A)	(A)
Fuel and Chemical Laboratory Technicians	(A)	x	x	x	x
Graphic Designers and Illustrators	x	x		x	x
Heating and Cooling Mechanics	(A)	x	x	x	(A)
Heavy Equipment Mechanics	(A)	x	x	x	(A)
Infantrymen (#)	x				x
Intelligence Specialists	x	x	x	x	x
Interpreters and Translators	x	x		x	x
Ironworkers	(A)			x	
Legal Technicians	x	x		x	x
Line Installers and Repairers	(A)	x	x	x	(A)
Lodging Specialists	x	x	x	x	x
Machinists	(A)	x	x	(A)	x
Maintenance Data Analysts	x	x	x	x	x
Mapping Technicians	(A)	x		x	x
Marine Engine Mechanics	(A)	x	x	(A)	x
Medical Laboratory Technicians	x	x	x	x	
Medical Record Technicians	x	x	x	x	
Medical Service Technicians	x	x	x	x	
Military Police	x	x	x	x	x
Motion Picture Camera Operators	(A)	x	x	(A)	x
Musicians	x	x	x	x	x
Non-Destructive Testers		x		x	x
Nursing Technicians	x	x		x	
Occupational Therapists	x	x	x	x	
Office Machine Repairers	(A)			(A)	x
Operating Room Technicians	x	x	x	x	
Opticians	x			x	
Optometric Technicians	x	x		x	
Ordnance Mechanics	(A)	x	x	x	x
Orthopedic Technicians	x	x		x	
Orthotic Specialists	x	x			
Paving Equipment Operators	(A)	x		x	x
Payroll Specialists	x	x	x	x	x
Personnel Specialists	x	x	x	x	x
Petroleum Supply Specialists	(A)	x	x	x	x
Pharmacy Technicians	x	x	x	x	
Photographers	(A)	x	x	(A)	x
Photographic Equipment Repairers	(A)	x		(A)	x
Photoprocessing Specialists	(A)	x		(A)	x
Physical Therapy Specialists	x	x	x	x	
Plumbers and Pipefitters	(A)	x	x	x	(A)
Postal Specialists	x	x	x	x	x
Power Plant Electricians	(A)	x	x	x	(A)
Power Plant Operators	(A)	x	x	x	x
Powerhouse Mechanics	(A)	x	x	x	
Precision Instrument Repairers	(A)	x		(A)	x
Printing Specialists	(A)	x		(A)	(A)
Quartermasters (Helmsmen)	x	x	x	x	

No. of Jobs	Annual Rqmnt.	ASVAB Scores		Training (Weeks)	DOL %
47,700	7,000	HS&T	29–35	9–14	33%
4,420	670	HS&T	39–48	2–13	
1,640	180	HS&T	38–47	12	26%
10,100	1,010	M&C	45–52	8–22	33%
12,900	2,410	M&C	39–45	8–29	29%
112,400	22,700	HS&T	42–50	8 Basic/8 Adv	
12,400	1,530	HS&T	35–45	9–24	
6,100	1,130	HS&T	39–48	7–20	
960	130	M&C	40–50	7– 8	39%
2,540	260	B&C	68–83	6– 8	94%
11,000	2,020	E&E	32–37	8–12	27%
2,950	300	B&C	34–43	OJT	23%
5,500	560	M&C	52–62	10–10	26%
11,100	1,280	B&C	43–50	4–15	
2,360	220	HS&T	27–38	9–14	
11,900	1,550	M&C	49–57	9–24	28%
7,300	650	HS&T	35–45	12–36	40%
7,300	730	HS&T	33–41	6–18	43%
38,200	7,700	HS&T	37–46	16–54	47%
64,860	14,400	HS&T	37–42	8–12	8%–47%
1,150	120	HS&T	28–37	7–14	
5,400	610	HS&T	48–70	11–24	25%
1,380	90	M&C	38–55	9–13	
12,300	1,460	HS&T	37–48	7–40	35%
200	30	HS&T	39–47	25–31	60%
470	60	M&C	38–48	12–22	72%
3,000	300	HS&T	37–46	8–26	40%
390	40	HS&T	44–55	21–26	
710	90	HS&T	38–52	9–13	25%
53,300	6,700	E&E	37–42	15–25	
470	60	HS&T	38–48	12	40%
130	20	HS&T	39–48	50–52	40%
3,580	640	M&C	38–50	4– 8	
10,000	1,080	B&C	48–58	6– 8	
27,600	3,210	B&C	48–58	7– 9	23%
12,700	2,660	M&C	38–47	4– 8	
12,500	1,490	HS&T	37–48	12–17	27%
2,300	230	HS&T	40–47	7–22	18%
4,050	420	E&E	27–40	9–32	
1,870	220	HS&T	32–40	12–24	
680	85	HS&T	38–48	11–28	58%
4,340	600	M&C	40–50	8–12	34%
4,140	630	B&C	44–55	3– 4	18%
1,330	210	E&E	38–47	4–17	32%
20,700	2,070	E&E	40–46	20–25	
9,500	950	E&E	45–52	12–24(Non-nuclear)	25+%
8,900	1,050	E&E	44–50	12–34	
1,780	200	HS&T	29–38	8–20	
4,290	430	HS&T	39–45	6–12	

Military Occupation	ARMY	USAF	USCG	NAVY	MARINES
Radar and Sonar Operators (#)	x	x	x	x	x
Radar and Sonar Repairers	(A)	x	x	(A)	(A)
Radio and TV Announcers	x	x	x	x	x
Radio Equipment Repairers	(A)	x		x	(A)
Radio Intelligence Operators	x	x		x	x
Radio Operators	(A)	x	x	x	x
Radiologic (X-Ray) Technicians	x	x	x	x	x
Recreation Specialists	x	x			x
Recruiting Specialists	x	x	x	x	x
Religious Program Specialists	x	x		x	
Reporters and Newswriters	x	x	x	x	x
Respiratory Therapists	x	x		x	
Riggers	(A)		x	x	x
Sales and Stock Specialists		x	x	x	x
Seamen	x	x	x	x	x
Secretaries and Stenographers	x		x	x	x
Sheet Metal Workers	(A)	x	x	x	(A)
Ship Electricians			x	(A)	
Shipfitters	(A)		x	x	
Shipping & Receiving Specialists	x	x	x	x	x
Space Systems Specialists		x		x	
Special Operations Forces (#)	x	x		x	x
Stock & Inventory Specialists	x	x	x	x	x
Surveying Technicians	(A)	x	x	x	(A)
Survival Equipment Specialists	x	x	x	x	x
Tank Crew Members (#)	x				x
Telephone Operators	(A)	x		x	x
Telephone Technicians	(A)	x	x	x	(A)
Teletype Operators	(A)	x	x	x	x
Teletype Repairers	(A)	x	x	x	(A)
Trainers	x	x	x	x	x
Transportation Specialists	x	x	x	x	x
Truck Drivers	x	x	x	x	x
Water & Sewage Treatment Plant Operators	(A)	x	x	x	(A)
Weather Observers	x	x	x	(A)	x
Welders	(A)	x	x	x	(A)
Well Drillers	(A)			x	x

(#) – No direct civilian equivalent; some skills and training may be useful in a variety of civilian jobs.

No. of Jobs	Annual Rqmnt.	ASVAB Scores		Training (Weeks)	DOL %
11,100	1,070	E&E	48–58	7–12	
25,700	2,680	E&E	44–50	20–30	
460	50	HS&T	57–67	10–12	28%
50,000	5,900	E&E	45–52	25–40	27%
15,800	2,980	E&E	37–48	17–24	
45,000	6,500	E&E	33–47	10–15	
3,350	360	HS&T	37–48	12–19	43%
1,130	80	HS&T	27–34	OJT	23%
12,900	1,290	HS&T	39–47	4–6	
1,380	210	B&C	50–61	7–8	
2,570	260	HS&T	50–67	9–11	29–35%
300	30	HS&T	37–50	32–41	45%
4,770	590	M&C	38–46	7–12	
4,080	410	B&C	34–45	6– 8	27–40%
96,900	54,900	M&C	49–62	6–12 + OJT	
2,130	220	B&C	55–65	6–10	29%
3,190	440	M&C	38–45	4– 8	46%
4,080	410	E&E	57–63	18–25	32%
1,840	190	M&C	42–50	10–13	
30,500	4,030	B&C	31–37	3– 8	18%
5,700	800	E&E	48–67	17–30	
6,100	1,430	HS&T	55–65	up to 72	
71,500	10,300	B&C	29–36	4–6	18%
4,740	750	HS&T	43–55	10–31	43%
7,700	960	M&C	40–50	9–12	
24,800	5,100	M&C	43–52	6–9	
10,500	1,820	HS&T	37–47	12–22	8%
12,100	2,130	E&E	44–50	10–38	28%
28,700	5,100	E&E	45–55	9–15	
14,800	1,480	E&E	48–57	20–30	61%
20,000	4,000	HS&T	34–42	2–14	
5,900	660	B&C	42–50	6– 9	29%
30,600	6,200	M&C	43–52	7– 9	17–24%
2,640	430	M&C	38–42	8–10	
5,300	630	HS&T	44–50	7–18	14%
6,400	640	M&C	38–45	8–12	21%
1,210	200	M&C	35–45	8	

Appendix **D**

Selected Colleges and Universities With ROTC Programs

The original plan for this book was to include a listing of every college and university in the United States that hosts a Reserve Officers Training Program sponsored by the Army, the Air Force, or the Navy. Preliminary research quickly showed that about a thousand institutions are involved in the ROTC program.

More interesting is that the three services continue to negotiate for participation by even more colleges and universities.

Under the circumstances, it seemed that an exhaustive list would require more effort than it was worth; it could not be complete and authoritative because of constant changes.

Appendix D is, therefore, a compromise. The process of selection was simply that of choosing one or more from each state or territory that are among the best—or, at least, the best known. That procedure quickly revealed another surprising fact: All three services offer ROTC units at many of the largest universities and even at some of the venerable military colleges such as the Virginia Military Institute and The Citadel.

Two other facts emerged from sifting the mass of data on ROTC institutions. First, as a general rule, if one state university in a given state hosts the ROTC program, so do the others. You may not be thinking about applying to the University of California at Berkeley, but the fact that Berkeley hosts an ROTC program suggests that so do most of the other members of the California state university system.

Second, many of the better-known colleges and universities that have hosted ROTC programs for many years now have arrangements with other institutions in the locality so that their students can participate in the military program at the original "host" campus. Many of the institutions listed here have these so-called crosstown agreements with one or more excellent schools that are not listed. As one example: The Naval ROTC unit at the University of California at Berkeley has crosstown agreements with Stanford University, the University of California at Davis, and the University of San Francisco, and probably by now, with several others: the California State Universities at Hayward, Sacramento, and San Jose; San Francisco State University, San Jose State University, and the University of Santa Clara.

If you want to know the name and location of every college and university in your state that offers ROTC training, the appropriate ROTC unit (Army, Air Force, Navy) at a college near you can supply the information, or you may write directly to the national offices:

Army ROTC, PO Box 9000, Clifton, NJ 07015–9974
AFROTC/RRO, Maxwell AFB, AL 36112
NROTC Information, PO Box 500, Clifton, NJ 07015

SELECTED COLLEGES AND UNIVERSITIES WITH ROTC PROGRAMS

Institution/Location	ARMY	USAF	NAVY
Alabama			
Auburn University, Auburn	x	x	x
Tuskegee Institute, Tuskegee	x	x	
University of Alabama, University	x	x	
Alaska			
University of Alaska, Fairbanks	x		
Arizona			
Arizona State University, Tempe	x	x	
Northern Arizona University, Flagstaff	x	x	
University of Arizona, Tucson	x	x	x
Arkansas			
University of Arkansas, Fayetteville	x	x	
California			
San Diego State University, San Diego	x	x	x
University of California, Berkeley	x	x	x
University of California, Los Angeles	x	x	x
University of Southern California, Los Angeles	x	x	x
Colorado			
University of Colorado, Boulder	x	x	x
Connecticut			
University of Connecticut, Storrs	x	x	
Delaware			
University of Delaware, Newark	x	x	
District of Columbia			
Georgetown University	x		
George Washington University	x		x
Howard University	x	x	
Florida			
Florida A&M University, Tallahassee		x	x
Jacksonville University, Jacksonville			x

University of Florida, Gainesville	x	x	x
Georgia			
University of Georgia, Athens	x	x	
Georgia Institute of Technology, Atlanta		x	x
Guam			
University of Guam, Agana	x		
Hawaii			
University of Hawaii, Honolulu	x		
University of Hawaii, Manoa		x	
Idaho			
University of Idaho, Moscow	x	x	x
Illinois			
Illinois Institute of Technology, Chicago		x	x
Northwestern University, Evanston		x	x
Southern Illinois University, Carbondale	x		
University of Illinois, Urbana	x	x	
Indiana			
Indiana University, Bloomington	x	x	
Purdue University, West Lafayette	x	x	x
University of Notre Dame, Notre Dame	x	x	x
Iowa			
Iowa State University, Ames	x	x	x
University of Iowa, Iowa City	x	x	
Kentucky			
University of Kentucky, Lexington	x	x	
Louisiana			
Tulane University, New Orleans	x	x	x
Maine			
Maine Maritime Academy, Castine			x
University of Maine, Orono	x	x	
Maryland			
Johns Hopkins University, Baltimore	x	x	
University of Maryland, College Park		x	
Massachusetts			
Boston University, Boston	x	x	x
College of the Holy Cross, Worcester		x	x
Massachusetts Institute of Technology, Cambridge	x	x	x
University of Massachusetts, Amherst	x	x	
Michigan			
University of Michigan, Ann Arbor	x	x	x
Minnesota			
University of Minnesota, Minneapolis	x	x	x
Mississippi			
University of Mississippi, University	x	x	x
Missouri			
University of Missouri, Columbia	x	x	x
Washington University, St. Louis	x	x	
Montana			
Montana State University, Bozeman	x	x	
University of Montana, Missouia	x		
Nebraska			
University of Nebraska, Lincoln	x	x	x

Nevada			
University of Nevada, Reno	x		
New Hampshire			
University of New Hampshire, Durham	x	x	x
New Jersey			
Princeton University, Princeton	x	x	
Rutgers University, New Brunswick	x	x	
New Mexico			
University of New Mexico, Albuquerque		x	x
New York			
Cornell University, Ithaca	x	x	x
Rensselaer Polytechnic Institute, Troy	x	x	x
Syracuse University, Syracuse	x	x	
University of Rochester, Rochester			x
North Carolina			
Duke University, Durham	x	x	x
University of North Carolina, Chapel Hill		x	x
North Dakota			
North Dakota University of A&AS, Fargo	x	x	
University of North Dakota, Grand Forks	x		
Ohio			
Bowling Green State University, Bowling Green	x	x	
Miami University, Oxford		x	x
Ohio State University, Columbus	x	x	x
Oklahoma			
University of Oklahoma, Norman	x	x	x
Oregon			
Oregon State University, Corvallis	x	x	x
Pennsylvania			
Pennsylvania State University, University Park	x	x	x
University of Pennsylvania, Philadelphia	x		x
Villanova University, Villanova			x
Puerto Rico			
University of Puerto Rico, Mayaguez	x	x	
Rhode Island			
University of Rhode Island, Kingston	x		
South Carolina			
The Citadel, Charleston	x	x	x
University of South Carolina, Columbia	x	x	
South Dakota			
University of South Dakota, Vermillion	x		
South Dakota State University, Brookings	x	x	
Tennessee			
Memphis State University, Memphis	x	x	x
Vanderbilt University, Nashville	x		x
Texas			
Rice University, Houston			x
Texas A&M University, College Station	x	x	x
Texas Technological Insitute, Lubbock	x	x	x
University of Texas, Austin	x	x	x
Utah			
University of Utah, Salt Lake City	x	x	x

Brigham Young University, Provo	x	x	
Vermont			
Norwich University, Norwich	x	x	x
University of Vermont, Burlington	x	x	
Virginia			
Hampton Institute, Hampton	x		x
University of Virginia, Charlottesville	x	x	x
Virginia Military Institute, Lexington	x	x	x
Virginia Polytechnic Institute, Blacksburg	x	x	x
Washington			
University of Washington, Seattle	x	x	x
Washington State University, Pullman	x	x	
West Virgina			
West Virgina University, Morgantown	x	x	
Wisconsin			
Marquette University, Milwaukee	x		x
University of Wisconsin, Madison	x	x	x
Wyoming			
University of Wyoming, Laramie	x	x	

Appendix **E**

For More Information

A great deal of useful information and details about various military recruitment and career programs can be found in your school or public library. Guidance counselors also have much information.

Recruiting offices are a good source of specific information if there is one nearby. Do not be afraid to ask questions.

If there is no recruiting office in your area, you can usually obtain the information you want by telephone or mail. In most cases headquarters for recruiting districts can be reached by toll-free "800" numbers; look in your telephone book under the United States Government section or request the number from "800" Directory Service. Post offices often have brochures that include tear-out inquiry cards already addressed to the appropriate service.

For information about specific programs, a number of such addresses are provided below.

1. *Service Academies*: Information about appointment procedures and study programs at the various service academies must usually be requested by mail. Send your inquiry, as desired, to:

Director of Admissions, United States Military Academy, West Point, NY 10996

Dean of Admissions, United States Naval Academy, Annapolis, MD 21402

Director of Cadet Admissions, United States Air Force Academy, Colorado Springs, CO 80840

Director of Admissions, United States Coast Guard Academy, New London, CT 06320

2. Reserve Officers Training Corps Programs (ROTC)

Army: Army ROTC, PO Box 9000, Clifton, NJ 07015
Air Force: AFROTC/ROR, Maxwell AFB, AL 36112
Navy: NROTC Information, PO Box 500, Clifton, NJ 07015

3. Officer Candidate Schools: Local recruiters, except for Coast Guard: Commandant (PTP-2), U.S. Coast Guard, Washington, DC 20591.

4. Programs for Students in Medical and Health Fields

U.S. Army Medical Education Support Agency, Attention: SGPE-PD, 1900 Half Street SW, Washington, DC 20234
Chief, Bureau of Medicine and Surgery, Department of the Navy, Washington, DC 20372
HQ AFMPC/SGEP, Randolph Air Force Base, TX 78150
Admissions Office, Uniformed Services University of Health Sciences, 4301 Jones Bridge Road, Bethesda, MD 20014

5. Direct Appointments in Medical and Allied Health Fields

Same as 4, above, except for U.S. Coast Guard: Commandant (G-PTP), U.S. Coast Guard Headquarters, Washington, DC 20590

6. Direct Appointments in Fields Other Than Medicine and Allied Health

a. Chaplain Programs
   Office of the Chief of Chaplains, Department of the Army, Washington, DC 20310
   Office of the Chief of Chaplains (OPO 1114), Department of the Navy, Washington, DC 20370
   Command Chaplain, AFMPC/HC, Randolph AFB, TX 78150
b. Judge Advocate General Programs
   Office of the Judge Advocate General, Attn: Personnel Plans and Training, Department of the Army, Washington, DC 20310
   Office of the Judge Advocate General, HQ U.S. Air Force, Attn: JAEC, Washington, DC 20330
   Commandant (G-PTP), U.S. Coast Guard Headquarters, Washington, DC 20590
   Note: Information on Navy programs: Navy recruiters

7. Programs for Students in Chaplaincy and Legal Fields

a. Chaplain Candidate Programs
   Office of the Chief of Chaplains, Department of the Army, Washington, DC 20314
   Office of the Chief of Chaplains (OPO1H4), Assistant for

Recruitment, Department of the Navy, Washington, DC 20370

Command Chaplain, ARPC/HC, Denver, CO 80280 (Air Force)

b. Judge Advocate General Programs

Office of the Judge Advocate General, Attn: Personnel Plans and Training, Department of the Army, Washington, DC 20310 (or, Army ROTC units at colleges and universities)

Commandant of the Marine Corps, Code MRRO, Washington, DC 20380

Office of the Judge Advocate General, HQ U.S. Air Force, Washington, DC 20314

Navy: Local recruiting stations.

INDEX

355
Mac   Macdonald, Robert W.
         Exploring careers in
         the military services

DATE DUE			
FEB 9			
SEP 18			
NOV 21			
DEC 2 0 P.M.			
MAR 1 0			
FEB 1			
22097			
3/28			

169   89

MEDIALOG INC
ALEXANDRIA, KY 41001